The Helsinki Process
and the Future of Europe

by the bishop over his congregation at Mass on the church's principal feast days. The book was written for him by a Winchester monk called Godeman, who included in it a long dedicatory poem in Latin. It contains 28 full-page miniatures (several more are now missing) and decorated initial pages introducing the most important blessings. The miniatures portray scenes from the life of Christ and some of saints. This manuscript is the chief example of the work of the 'Winchester school' of illumination, which flourished in England during the late 10th and early 11th centuries, and one of the greatest of all English medieval works of art.

Additional MS 49598

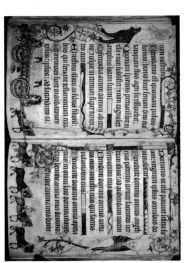

The Luttrell Psalter

Scenes of medieval life drawn from the pages of the Luttrell Psalter have enlivened countless books of social history. The manuscript was made in the early 14th century for Sir Geoffrey Luttrell of Irnham, in Lincolnshire, who died in 1345. He and his wife Agnes (d. 1340), with their daughter-in-law, are portrayed in the book, which is outstanding for the wealth and detail of its marginal illustration. Many different aspects of the farming activities on Sir Geoffrey's estates are lovingly depicted. Such characters as the elderly ploughman and the boy herding geese were surely directly inspired from real life. The Luttrell household staff is shown, preparing to serve a banquet in the great hall of the manor, and on other pages bear baiting, dancing and backgammon remind the onlooker of the lighter side of life in Lincolnshire in the 1330s.

Additional MS 42130

manuscript during the 8th century by an anchorite called Billfrith and an Anglo-Saxon gloss, the earliest known translation of the Gospels into any form of the English language, was supplied in the 10th century by Aldred, provost of Chester-le-Street. Intricate patterns painted in soft bright colours fill the principal pages of this marvellous book. Many of them are woven from the elongated bodies of birds and beasts and one, on the opening page of Luke's Gospel, includes an extremely characterful cat.

Cotton MS Nero D.iv

The Grandval Bible

The Grandval Bible was made at the Benedictine Abbey of Tours in the second quarter of the 9th century. It is one of a series of mammoth bibles produced by the Tours scriptorium at this time. Approximately twenty different scribes worked on this particular book and its production required the skins of between two and three hundred sheep, which gives some idea of the scale of the operation. Tours boasted a particularly good text of the Latin Bible, revised by their abbot, the English scholar Alcuin of York (d. 804), at the request of the Emperor Charlemagne. The manuscript contains four full-page illustrations, influenced by late classical models. During the Middle Ages it was at the monastery of Moutier-Grandval in the diocese of Basle, from which it takes its name.

Additional MS 10546

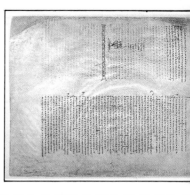

was for 300 years in the Patriarchal Library of Alexandria, was presented in 1627 to Charles I by Cyril Lucar, the calvinistic Patriarch of Constantinople. The gift was made in gratitude for the assistance of Sir Thomas Roe, the British Ambassador to the Sublime Porte, against the intrigues of the French Ambassador. The manuscript's arrival caused great excitement and sparked off intensive study of the Greek text of the New Testament. It was naturally the first manuscript to be rescued from the fire in 1731 at Ashburnham House (allegedly 'safer from fire' than its previous home), which so seriously damaged the manuscripts of Sir Thomas Cotton.

Royal MS I D.VIII

Magna Carta

Although Magna Carta has come to be regarded as the cornerstone of liberty in the English-speaking world, it does not contain any sweeping statement of principle. It is a series of detailed concessions about the law and feudal rights wrung from an unwilling King John by his baronial opponents in 1215. The Magna Carta display contains six documents associated with the grant of the charter. Item 2 is the actual document summarising the barons' demands to which King John set his seal at Runnymede on 15 June 1215. This document was cast into a more correct legal form by the royal chancery to produce the first authoritative text of Magna Carta. Items 3 and 4 are two copies of this text, one of which was probably sent to the Cinque Ports. The recipient of the other is unknown.

Cotton MS Augustus ii. 106

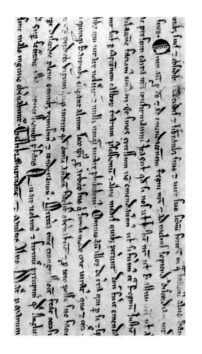

major fugue, no. 17, written wholly in Bach's hand, is shown.

Additional MS 35021

Jane Eyre

Jane Eyre was Charlotte Brontë's second novel, but the first to be published. She completed the fair copy (now in the British Library) in August 1847, and sent it to Smith, Elder and Co., the only publishing house to write her an encouraging letter about her earlier work, *The Professor*. It is remarkably neat, with relatively few corrections, and a beautiful example of what Charlotte's biographer, Mrs Gaskell, described as her 'clear, legible, delicate traced writing'. The story of passionate love checked by stern moral scruples and beset to the end by apparently insurmountable difficulties was published two months later, to almost instant success. Critics seized upon its imaginative power and the 'reality' and 'freshness' of its style; Thackeray, to whom Charlotte dedicated the second edition, 'lost a whole day in reading it'. It remains one of the most popular and widely read of English novels.

Additional MS 43474

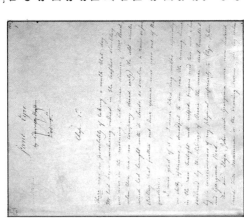

Produced by Exhibitions & Education Service
The British Library, Great Russell Street, London WC1B 3DG
© The British Library Board 1984. Printed in Great Britain.

WHAT TO SEE: MANUSCRIPTS

DEC PG

The Harley Golden Gospels

The Harley Golden Gospels is one of a series of richly illuminated Gospel books produced at the court workshop of the Emperor Charlemagne about 800. Its text is written entirely in gold and every page is decorated, the most elaborate schemes being reserved for the canon tables and the opening pages of each of the four gospels. The style of illumination evolved for these de luxe books drew heavily upon the influence of late classical work available to the artists of the time and also upon the work of English illuminators of earlier generations, some of whose books had been transported to the European continent during the 8th century by missionaries working among the heathen Germanic tribes. Magnificent copies of the gospels were of great psychological importance during the early years of conversion, because they represented the church's message in visible and splendid form.

Harley MS 2788

The Benedictional of St Ethelwold

Ethelwold, Bishop of Winchester (d. 984) was the original owner of this magnificent volume, which

The Bedford Hours

The Bedford Hours, one of the most lavishly decorated of the many splendid manuscripts produced in Paris at the beginning of the 15th century, belonged to John, Duke of Bedford, brother of King Henry V of England, and his wife, Anne of Burgundy. It was probably made to celebrate their marriage in 1423. Bedford was Regent of France for his infant nephew, Henry VI, to whom the Duchess gave the book as a Christmas present in 1430, and Anne was the sister of his most important ally, the Duke of Burgundy. The manuscript contains 38 large miniatures and more than 1,200 small ones, set off on every page by immensely elaborate floral borders, delicately painted in gold and bright colours.

Additional MS 18850

The Lindisfarne Gospels

The Lindisfarne Gospels, written and illuminated in Northumbria at the end of the 7th century 'in honour of God and St Cuthbert', is the earliest great master-piece of English book decoration. A 10th-century inscription added to the last page tells us that the book was made by Eadfrith, Bishop of Lindisfarne 698–721, and bound by his successor Ethelwald. Both were monks of the Lindisfarne community in Cuthbert's own lifetime and the Gospels was probably prepared for the celebration of his formal elevation to sainthood in 698. Jewelled ornaments

The Codex Sinaiticus

This is one of the two earliest complete Bibles in Greek (the other is in the Vatican Library). It was in the Monastery of St Catherine in Sinai for a thousand years. Constantine Tischendorf recognized it as 'the pearl of all his researches' and managed to have it transferred to the Czar of Russia in 1859. In 1933 the Soviet Union sold it to Britain at the bargain price of £100,000. Amid tremendous excitement, over £60,000 was raised by public subscription. It has lost half of its Old Testament, but is otherwise in magnificent condition, and beautifully legible.

Additional MS 43725

The Codex Alexandrinus

Beowulf

This Anglo-Saxon epic poem, one of the most famous works of English medieval literature, is known only from the British Library copy, written out in about AD 1000. It celebrates the deeds of a hero of much older times, Beowulf the Goth, who as a young man single-handedly slays the monster Grendel, followed by Grendel's evil mother, and many years later destroys a marauding fire-dragon, receiving his own death-wound in the fight. Scholars still hold varying opinions about its original date and provenance, although it is generally agreed that the poem was composed 300-400 years earlier than the making of this copy. It cannot be earlier than the introduction of Christianity into Saxon England, which began with the mission of St Augustine in AD 598, since a strong Christian flavour pervades the entire work.

Cotton MS Vitellius A.xv

Letter of Queen Elizabeth I

This letter, written in 1594 to King James VI of Scotland, shows the prose style and handwriting of Elizabeth I at their most fluent and expressive. It is one of an important series of letters from Elizabeth to James, all written by the queen herself without the aid of a secretary. The correspondence brings out the complexity of the relationship between the two monarchs: although Elizabeth had reluctantly agreed to the execution of James's mother, Mary Queen of Scots, in 1587, it was James who was chosen to succeed to the throne of England, as James I, in 1603.

The display of English Historical Documents also includes a letter of Elizabeth when young to her brother King Edward VI.

Additional MS 23240

Johann Sebastian Bach, *The Well-Tempered Clavier*

Bach's 48 preludes and fugues – which take their name from the system of tuning keyboard instruments in equal temperament – are among the greatest works in the repertory. As familiar, and accessible, to the modern pianist as to players of the instruments of Bach's day, they are arranged in two sets, each using all of the keys. The British Library manuscript has all but three of the preludes and fugues of the second set and was written out by Bach, with the help of his second wife Anna

The Helsinki Process and the Future of Europe

Edited by Samuel F. Wells, Jr.

Foreword by Ambassador Max M. Kampelman

Woodrow Wilson Center Special Studies, No. 1

WW THE WILSON CENTER PRESS   WASHINGTON, DC

Woodrow Wilson Center Special Studies, No. 1

The Wilson Center Press
1000 Jefferson Drive, S.W.
Washington, D.C. 20560 U.S.A.

©1990 by the Woodrow Wilson International Center for Scholars

Printed in the United States of America

♾ Printed on acid-free paper

9 8 7 6 5 4 3 2 1

Library of Congress Cataloging-in-Publication Data

The Helsinki Process and the future of Europe / edited by Samuel F.
  Wells, Jr.
    p.   cm.—(Woodrow Wilson Center special studies : no. 1)
  Based on papers delivered at a conference of experts held at the
  Woodrow Wilson International Center for Scholars in April 1990.
  Includes bibliographical references.
  ISBN 0-943875-29-3 (alk. paper)
  1. Conference on Security and Cooperation in Europe (1975
Helsinki, Finland)—Congresses. 2. Security, International—
Congresses. 3. European cooperation—Congresses. 4. Human rights—
Europe—Congresses. 5. Europe—Military policy—Congress.
I. Wells, Samuel F. II. Woodrow Wilson International Center for
Scholars. III. Series.
JX1393.C65H446   1990
327.1'7'094—dc20   90-12854
                                                       CIP

Contents

Acknowledgments

In the production of anything as complicated as a conference leading to a published volume, many people play a role. Given the complexity of the subject and the speed with which the conference was organized and the book published, the number of people involved and the need to express appreciation to them are both greater.

This project originated in discussions among the senior staff of the Woodrow Wilson Center about the need to use our experience and large number of well-positioned Fellows to contribute to a better understanding of the changes taking place in Europe. Charles Blitzer, the Center's director, urged us to organize a major meeting on the future of Europe, and he supported this project strongly from the beginning.

Our decision to focus on the Conference on Security and Cooperation in Europe (CSCE) and its potential role in shaping a future Europe resulted from a conversation in December of 1989 between Robert Blackwill, Special Assistant to the President for European and Soviet Affairs, and Renata Fritsch-Bournazel, a former Guest Scholar of the Center and member of our West European Advisory Council. Helping at every stage of the way to implement the general concept of a conference on the CSCE and the future of Europe were my senior staff colleagues Michael H. Haltzel of West European Studies, John R. Lampe of East European Studies, and Robert S. Litwak of International Studies.

The Center is also greatly indebted to Ambassador Max M. Kampelman, a member and former chairman of our Board of Trustees, for his contribution to the design of the conference and for chairing it throughout its two days. Ambassador Kampelman also took the time from his demanding preparations for the CSCE Conference on the Human Dimension in Copenhagen to prepare a foreword for the volume. We are indebted to John Evans of the Department of State, a former Guest Scholar at the Woodrow Wilson Center, who provided us with extensive advice on issues and personnel to involve in the conference and who participated in the meeting himself. The authors and commentators who made the conference such a

ix

stimulating and informative two days all took their assignments seriously and met their responsibilities fully. We could not have proceeded without them, and we are very much in their debt.

We are equally indebted, as anyone who has put a meeting of this sort together will appreciate, to our sources of financial support. David Hamburg and Frederic Mosher of the Carnegie Corporation of New York provided prompt and generous support, and Enid Schoettle and Stanley Heginbotham of the Ford Foundation graciously allowed the use of funds for this conference that had been initially approved for a somewhat different purpose. We hope that our funding supporters, all of whom share a deep interest in this subject, will be pleased with the published results of the conference.

I must also thank several members of my immediate staff for doing all of the logistical and coordinating work involved in staging an international conference as well as for doing the major work in completing the manuscript. Deep and special thanks go to Jane Mutnick, Monica Marsolais, and Constantine Symeonides-Tsatsos. We also appreciate the special emergency help provided by our colleagues Maria Holperin, Angela Carter, and Charlotte Thompson.

The staff of the Wilson Center Press deserves special thanks for their efficient and timely support of this project and for their creative efforts to introduce our new rapid format of Woodrow Wilson Center Special Studies to accommodate the need for prompt publication. Warmest thanks go to Glenn W. LaFantasie, director of the Wilson Center Press, and managing editor Joseph F. Brinley, Jr.

S.F.W.

Foreword

Max M. Kampelman

The ideals of freedom and democracy have seldom been more in the news than in the year beginning in July of 1989. Indeed, the latest authoritative Freedom House annual survey shows that 1989 was the freest year since that organization, which I have the honor to chair, began its monitoring effort in 1955. By Freedom House standards, sixty-one countries and fifty territories are "free," governing more than 2 billion people. In addition, there are fifty-four countries and three territories in which 1.2 billion people live with a relatively high but lesser degree of freedom.

Probably at no time since 1918–1919, when Woodrow Wilson was leading the drive for an open and democratic peace settlement following World War I including the creation of a collective security system based on the League of Nations, have the concepts of freedom and democracy been so widely discussed. The revolutions of 1989 in eastern Europe responded to this same deep human desire for freedom that the people of those regions had indeed expressed in 1918 and 1919, when they were in many cases initially becoming free from the Russian and Austro-Hungarian empires.

The evidence is strong that the Helsinki process played a very constructive role in fueling the aspirations and building the contacts which helped produce the revolutions of 1989. It is entirely appropriate that the center for advanced research that is our nation's memorial to Woodrow Wilson held on April 23–24, 1990, a major international conference on "Helsinki II and the Future of Europe." I had the privilege of chairing that Woodrow Wilson International Center for Scholars conference and was very impressed with the papers and discussion that dominated two days. I am convinced that these issues are of high importance both to the public and the governments of all the European nations and the United States and Canada. I hope that the message of this book will be read widely and taken to heart.

The Helsinki Final Act of 1975 was not always viewed as favorably in the United States as it is today. When President Gerald Ford signed it in 1975, critics argued that the human rights provisions, which were strongly supported by the United States, would turn out to be mere rhetoric—-ignored by all nations. The critics feared that the formalization of European boundaries, which made the Baltic States satellites of the Soviet Union and served largely Soviet interests, would survive and prevail. While this was a fair concern, it turned out to be unfounded. But criticism continued. During the 1980 presidential campaign, candidate Ronald Reagan asked why the United States should attend the Madrid meetings to evaluate the Helsinki Final Act. Yet we were able in Madrid to make good progress, and I am glad that when President Carter asked me to lead the American delegation to that Madrid conference, I accepted. I would also note that when Reagan assumed the office of President in January 1981, he asked me to continue as head of our delegation, and I did so.

At the Madrid conference we began to see real progress in human rights within the Helsinki process. In concert with our European allies, we contended that the words and promises of the Helsinki Final Act should be taken seriously by all of the thirty-five countries that signed it. We served notice that it reflected the criteria to which all nations should aspire and by which states were to be judged. Despite a reluctance on the part of some European countries, the United States believed that we should sharpen our emphasis on human rights standards and demonstrate that our concerns were more than rhetorical. We acted on our belief that we were obligated to evaluate and to criticize openly violations of human rights by the Soviet Union and its satellites.

At first, the Soviet Union insisted that the discussion of human rights behavior amounted to interference in its internal affairs and was thus clearly improper. Our response, equally insistent, was that if the Soviets would not live up to their human rights commitment, they could not expect us to trust them to live up to any other international commitments they made.

When the Soviets in Madrid began to criticize the United States and western human rights behavior, we responded by welcoming their acceptance of this as a legitimate agenda item and by answering the criticism. The legitimacy of human rights for full discussion as part of the conference's agenda was thereby established. At Madrid we intensified the discussion and went beyond generalities. The United States and its allies cited the names of victims of oppression and strongly condemned the violations. We made the meetings personal, replacing theoretical discussion with evidence of irrefutable wrongs against specific human beings, not just "humanity" in general. When the Madrid meeting ended in September 1983, the statement on human rights was made even stronger. And even that document was toughened at the conclusion of the most recent meeting in Vienna last year.

The effects of the Madrid meeting were not just felt in the Soviet Union and the Warsaw Pact. A number of western foreign ministers have told me that the wide dissemination of cases of individual human rights violations in Europe helped to create the climate for West European acceptance of NATO's Pershing II and cruise missiles during the Euromissile dispute of the early 1980s. That, in turn, was subsequently of inestimable value in arriving at an intermediate-range nuclear forces agreement on arms control signed by Presidents Reagan and Gorbachev in December of 1987. The events of Madrid also had an important effect among opponents of the communist regimes in eastern Europe. Large numbers of the men and women who led the revolutions of 1989 and now have central places in the emerging democratic governments provide moving testimony to the hope and support which they derived from the Helsinki process and its investigations into the way in which human rights were being violated. The Madrid conference proved to be a turning point for the Helsinki process. It won strong support in the United States and proved to be a broadly recognized statement of human rights standards to which nations should aspire and against which the behavior of nations should be judged.

The movement of reform in the Soviet Union today and the revolutions in eastern Europe provide new challenges for the Helsinki process. We must advance human rights and there are many opportunities to do so, especially in the countries of southeastern Europe and in the Soviet Union. As a recent conference on the economic components of the Helsinki process shows, there is an immense range of work to be done in opening economic opportunity and in supporting the principles of free economies. Finally, the Helsinki process must use its security provisions to give eastern Europe and the Soviet Union a better sense of protection at a time when the West appears victorious and the Warsaw Pact has become impotent and irrelevant. These security provisions can provide the basis for discussion of border and ethnic conflicts in the nations of eastern Europe and the institution of crisis prevention regimes, set arms control terms and supervise verification, and provide a general forum in which political dialogue and cooperation can be stimulated.

In relation to these security issues within the Helsinki process, I want to point out that contrary to much discussion in the United States, the Helsinki process does not compete for authority with the Atlantic alliance. The Conference on Security and Cooperation in Europe (CSCE)—the formal name for the Helsinki process—includes all of the nations of Europe, except for Albania as of now, plus the United States and Canada. It will talk about the political-military dimensions of security, not the issues of force structure and armaments. The CSCE is a loose and informal set of conferences at present. There are many suggestions for its reform to create a small institutional base with which it could provide continuing supervision for agreements. But the CSCE will never be in the business of providing basic defense for the West. That will remain the job of the North Atlantic Treaty Organization (NATO), and there is no inherent conflict between the roles of the CSCE and NATO.

In looking at the prospects and opportunities for the Helsinki process, I would like very much to associate myself with the remarks of Congressman Steny Hoyer, the co-chairman of the U.S. Commission on Security and Cooperation in Europe. Congressman Hoyer's dinner address to our conference participants and additional special guests is included as Chapter 17 of this book, and I especially commend it to you.

In a few days I leave for Copenhagen, where I have the privilege to serve as head of the U.S. delegation for the Conference on the Human Dimension within the Helsinki process.

We intend to advance ideas and proposals under which a universally accepted detailed "rule of law" concept will be incorporated as a norm for the responsible domestic behavior of nations. We are also looking at ways of assuring open political competition through political parties and free elections within states as a way of assuring stability, security, and peace among nations. Our job is far from completed, and we welcome the views of this book and the support of its readers in advancing the cause of freedom and democracy.

May 31, 1990

Chapter 1

An Overview

Elizabeth Pond

Managing the decay of Soviet power, the rise of German power, and the end of the whole post–World War II "cold war" system will be the most urgent international task for the 1990s. In past centuries such tectonic shifts regularly led to war. In today's world, however, the major players all agree, we must avoid war and find the institutions and habits that will ensure the peaceful nature even of the monumental change now occurring in Europe.

No single institution can by itself provide this assurance. The North Atlantic Treaty Organization (NATO), the European Community, the Council of Europe, the Conference on Security and Cooperation in Europe (CSCE), and other more or less familiar organizations must all temper confrontation and channel cooperation among nations if the transition to the post-postwar regime of European security is to avoid dangerous ruptures. And all these institutions must themselves evolve and adapt to the rush of events.

The newest, the most flexible—and certainly the most invisible—of these institutions is the Conference on Security and Cooperation in Europe, otherwise known as the "Helsinki process." With no bureaucracy and no central office, the CSCE is indeed a process—a series of ad hoc international conferences—rather than an organization. It is "a round table writ large," according to Representative Steny Hoyer, co-chairman of the U.S. Commission on Security and Cooperation in Europe, or a "group of people forced to come to consensus," as described by Ambassador George Vest, an American diplomat who was involved in the creation of the

1

CSCE. It was born in 1975, when all European states except for Albania joined with the Soviet Union, the United States, and Canada to pledge not to change existing borders by force and to cooperate in the future in economics and in promoting human rights.

The "Final Act" at Helsinki was not a treaty; it had no binding legal force. Yet it acted as a catalyst for profound change, both in setting standards of behavior in such areas as human rights and in giving East European nations a venue for diplomatic action autonomous from their Soviet patron. With a repeat summit of the thirty-five member states scheduled to take place at the end of 1990, CSCE now promises to do even more—to act as a buffer to the shocks of German unification and the shrinkage of Soviet empire.

The Soviet Union, in proposing the new summit, apparently hoped initially to see a CSCE regime replace NATO and the disintegrating Warsaw Treaty Organization. The Federal Republic of Germany, for its part, would like to obtain a CSCE blessing on German unification as a substitute for a formal peace treaty ending World War II—and thus avoid special "singular" restrictions on Germany as well as open-ended claims for reparations. Other Europeans would hope that the CSCE could institutionalize—and moderate—the Soviet voice in European security arrangements and help to integrate the emerging East European democracies into the European cooperative system. The U.S. government, suspicious of the Soviet notion of substituting CSCE for the existing alliances—and convinced that a dissolution of NATO would ensure the departure of U.S. forces from NATO Europe, even if this is no longer Moscow's intent—is reluctant to see an expanded role for CSCE without clearly defining its limits.

To explore the evolving roles of the Helsinki process in the very new era in Europe following the East European revolutions of 1989, the Woodrow Wilson International Center for Scholars sponsored a conference on April 23 and 24, 1990, covering three basic aspects of CSCE activity: security, economics, and legal safeguards of human and political rights. Chaired by Ambassador Max M. Kampelman, who headed the U.S. delegation to the CSCE Review Conference in Madrid from 1980 to 1983, the conference was held at a time when the future structure of Europe and the role of the CSCE were both under intense discussion. At a time of flux, when neither the

Soviet position on the external conditions for German unification nor the American position on CSCE itself had yet been decided, the Soviet and official American participants in the conference remained cautious in anticipating where a new summit might lead. Europeans from both western and Central Europe were more bold in envisaging how, in the "genius of overlapping institutions," as one participant expressed it, CSCE might facilitate the transition to the dynamic Europe of the 1990s.

Security

In security issues the sharpest contrast was offered by Viktor Shein, Director of Security Studies at the Institute for Europe in Moscow, and Michael Stürmer, Director of the Research Institute for International Affairs in the Federal Republic of Germany. Shein opposed NATO membership for a united Germany and called for a CSCE system to substitute for the old "bloc system, which won't work well in three, four, or five years." He argued that the West too should prefer having Germany out of NATO, in part because, he asserted, German membership is marginal to NATO and German public opinion is "negative" on the issue. Stürmer, on the contrary, asked if the Soviet Union really wanted to push Germany into seeking security on its own—including acquiring nuclear weapons and setting up an independent general staff that would not be integrated into the multinational NATO command.

Shein stood his ground and did not hint, as other Soviet officials and academics have done privately if not (yet) publicly, that Moscow would in the end find a Germany anchored to NATO less threatening than an unattached Germany.

Stürmer and others contended that with 600,000 Soviet troops remaining in Central Europe, NATO is still needed, albeit with a somewhat changed agenda. The enhanced warning time before any potential attack as these troops return to the Soviet Union over the next few years will remove the need for immediate forward defense of Germany by NATO military forces. The risks of crisis instability and hasty preemption will be heightened, however, as Soviet forces in the theater become too few to be a serious threat, but remain too many to ignore. As the balance between Germany and Russia shifts in Europe, Stürmer urges avoidance both of unstable German neutrality that could leave the country as a "loose cannon" and any reversion to a nineteenth-century balance of power pattern that by perpetuating four-power controls in Germany might possibly trigger future German revolt. Instead, he recommends a "benign stability" of continued American engagement in Europe to secure both East-West and West-West equilibrium and "turn the German question from a divisive burden to the engine of Europe." This course could also protect European neutrals from being "overshadowed" by the Soviet Union and would allow the European Community to nurture democracies in Central Europe as it did in Spain and Portugal in the 1970s. Harnessing German energies to NATO, Stürmer argues, should meet the "enlightened self-interest" of the Soviets.

In this context some discussants described CSCE as a face-saving device both for the Soviet Union and for West Germany. A CSCE system perceived as bridging rather than supplanting the present alliances would give Moscow a graceful cover for accepting German membership in NATO. At the same time it would let Bonn pledge the military restraint that both Germans and other Europeans desire without onerously "singularizing" Germany, since all CSCE nations would similarly pledge restraint.

Without explicitly opposing such a broad mandate for CSCE, an American diplomat dampened speculation by downplaying a security role and focusing instead on extending CSCE's role as a pacesetter from human rights to political rights. In a subsequent special address, Representative Steny Hoyer challenged this view in asserting that "the CSCE has not been the enemy of NATO." In the future, he argued, "NATO does not have to be threatened by the development of a European security system but could instead be promoted as an integral part of such a system."

Conceptually, retired British Royal Air Force Air Vice-Marshal R. A. Mason cautioned against either of two "polarities"—overhasty prescription of a formal European security system, or failure to provide any overarching system whatever. There is a paradoxical need, he suggested, "to provide for the eventuality of the Soviet Union being responsible for insecurity, while at the same time incorporating her into the system." In defining a role for the Helsinki process,

George Vest drew a distinction between "adding to an atmosphere helpful to security [which CSCE does] and producing the security itself [which CSCE does not]."

Georges Vaugier envisaged a central role for the European Community in moving toward European political union as recently proposed by France and West Germany. Rozanne Ridgway, President of the Atlantic Council, expressed skepticism toward grand designs either for CSCE or for a European Community autonomous of NATO in addressing European security. She welcomed CSCE participation in the "reassurance" and "psychological buttressing" that is needed during the present transition. But she warned against relegating the United States to wait-and-see passivity in which the Europeans would first make decisions and then expect Washington to provide the military contribution to implement them.

In presenting a view from the largest of Germany's Central European neighbors, Bronisław Geremek, Solidarity's floor leader in Poland's lower house, stressed the importance of formal acceptance of the post–World War II borders by the "European superpower" of the new Germany, whatever form final European settlement takes. He, too, strongly endorsed the need for a continuing American engagement in Europe to help solidify the democratic revolutions in Central Europe. He portrayed active American and West European involvement in the region less as restraining the Soviet Union than as helping it, in line with Andrei Sakharov's hope that the collapse of Soviet empire might spur democratic change inside the Soviet Union itself. He, like many participants, worried about the potential for nationalist clashes in Central Europe.

There was a consensus among participants from the countries of the western alliance that CSCE should not become an ambitious system of collective security on the model of the Kellogg-Briand Pact, since "if all are allied with all, nobody is allied with anyone." The Soviet participant did not explicitly address this issue. The Swiss ambassador to the United States, Edouard Brunner, was more open to the idea and thought that collective security might offer some assurance to the Central European nations, whose security is left uncertain as the old Warsaw Treaty Organization disintegrates.

A broadened CSCE could usefully perform nonmilitary security functions, all agreed, such as setting standards for advancing the rule of law in European states, expanding confidence-building measures, overseeing environmental and technological cooperation, and perhaps mediating in ethnic conflicts in Central Europe and the Balkans. More controversial would be any expanded direct role for CSCE in arms-control verification or—in the suggestion of Mason—sponsorship of a peacekeeping force from neutral European countries for possible dispatch to areas of tension in Central Europe. Brunner acknowledged that a peacekeeping force might be a "fitting" idea, but he noted the difficulties in securing approval for such an initiative through the complicated Swiss domestic political mechanism.

Opinions differed as to whether the CSCE should avoid setting up any bureaucracy or whether it might benefit from having a small permanent staff. Opinions also differed on whether or not voluntary CSCE commitments should be written into formal treaties.

Economics

In economics the conference viewed the primary task as providing economic underpinning for the fledgling Central European democracies. Democracy and economic prosperity are so closely linked in the expectations of the man in the street in Central Europe at this point that economic failure could produce democratic collapse as well. This danger is of more than academic interest to Europe as a whole, since it could quickly give rise to threats to security.

Professors Alan Milward of the London School of Economics and Josef Brada of Arizona State University presented pessimistic views of the myriad economic problems facing Central Europe, including constricting structures of trade dependency within the old Council for Mutual Economic Assistance (Comecon); distorted prices; low productivity; prospective unemployment as industry is forced to become competitive; huge debt loads for several countries and probable rescheduling for every nation in the region except for Czechoslovakia; inflationary pressures; rudimentary banking, accounting, and foreign trade structures; low purchasing power; lack of a sophisticated industrial sector ready to produce goods the West will want to buy; and reluctance of the West in any case to open its markets to Central European manufactures.

Milward, analyzing the role of the Marshall Plan for financing imports of capital goods in the economic recovery in western Europe after World War II, concluded that conditions differ so greatly between Central Europe today and western Europe in the 1940s that a Marshall Plan for Central Europe in the 1990s would probably not help much. Among other things he stressed the particular importance of West German exports to the rest of the region; within two years of the beginning of the Marshall Plan these exports were pivotal. He did not see an East Central European nation able to act as a similar pivot today. With some irony he also contrasted the much higher degree of government intervention in the European economies in the late 1940s with the high degree of free market operation that is now expected to prevail in Central Europe as the planning system is scrapped.

The West, Milward suggested, should not stimulate false hope in Central Europe and generate a "myth about the links between the Marshall Plan, foreign trade, and currency stabilization," and their relevance to Central Europe today. Nor, he added, should the West expect any Marshall Plan for Central Europe to "help to increase levels of employment" in Keynesian fashion in the West.

Brada described the fragility of Central European economies as they seek to shift from their previous orientation to Comecon toward western Europe. He expected the increase in pan-European trade and investment to have "positive effects," but he doubted whether the existing organizations set up to serve commercial intercourse in a divided Europe can adapt easily "to serve as a bridge between East and West." The new Bank for European Recovery and Development is "useful," but does not address key problems, he suggested. Privatization will occur only slowly, he anticipated, given the lack of "domestic financial systems capable of financing the purchases of state-owned assets" and an "imbalance between the capital stock and liquid savings." Price flexibility will be limited; capital markets are all but non-existent. And where countries have set up commercial banks, as in Hungary and Czechoslovakia, the banks have already issued many loans on the basis of criteria other than profitability.

Nor is the solution of having western investors buy up the major Central European firms a happy one. Western investment could generate local resentment at being taken over by foreigners, and that western investment could also gravitate toward an "Ivan Boesky approach" of exploiting distortions for short-term profit in ways that would not promote healthy economic adjustment.

In comments Jan Vanous, President of PlanEcon Research Associates, took a somewhat more optimistic view of prospects. He acknowledged the particular problems of tackling restructuring simultaneously in six or seven countries and the shock that may accompany swift unemployment of up to fifteen or twenty percent. He also doubted western commitment to opening markets to Central European exports, especially as the fading Soviet threat removes the sense of cold war urgency. But he found comparisons with the old Marshall Plan essentially irrelevant. He summed up the basic Central European need as more infrastructure, including financial institutions, accounting, communications, training, and education. Building such infrastructure will be costly and require time, and there is no lobby for it in the West, since the service lobby there is very weak. The infrastructure would evolve by itself over twenty years, he noted, but since it is needed in five years, it would be a good idea for the West to accelerate it with comprehensive Marshall Plan-type aid. Aid would clearly pay off for the West in such areas as cleaning up the filthy Central European environment; one Deutsche mark invested at the source of pollution in the German Democratic Republic or Czechoslovakia has the same impact in the Federal Republic as five Deutsche marks put into cleanup efforts in West Germany itself.

Hans W. Decker, President of Siemens Corporation in New York, describing his approach as "bottom-up," argued that private efforts can promote economic development in Central Europe better than a new governmental Marshall Plan. He did not directly challenge the pessimism of previous speakers, nor did he cite the widespread expectation by Germans of a new "economic miracle" in the German Democratic Republic in the next five years that would repeat West Germany's own economic miracle of the 1950s. From the point of view of a company that has been doing business in Central Europe for decades, however, he portrayed the real need as privatization, development of capital markets, and establishment of the proper legal framework for business. As these prerequisites are realized, he indicated, private enterprise will take over. He did contest the view that private companies would prefer to invest in western Europe for economies of scale; especially in his company's sector of industrial goods, he said, firms want to locate as close to their customers as possible and will therefore set up manufacturing plants in East Central Europe itself.

The conference perceived only a limited role for CSCE as such in the economic sphere. The CSCE conference on economics in Bonn in April 1990 endorsed broad (generally free-market) principles for economic development. Concrete investment, know-how, and markets, however, will depend less on CSCE proclamations than on decisions by the private sector and on willingness by the European Community to open its markets to Central European exports and eventually to accept Central European states as members. The most the CSCE could do would be to provide a general atmosphere of East-West cooperation that would not artificially hinder efforts by businessmen and multilateral organizations to draw Central European countries into the world trading system.

The most upbeat of any of the discussants was Hans-Peter Krueger, an economist from the German Democratic Republic. He thought the speakers focused unduly on the question of western help for Central Europe and neglected the will, the skill, and the readiness to take risks of the people in the region. He expected these people, including the East Germans, to solve their own problems. What he sought from the West above all—beyond investments in specific areas such as environmental cleanup—was high-quality teachers of management, accounting, and other business skills to help them get on with the job of reforming the economy.

Human and Political Rights

To gain a sense of how the Helsinki process might help shape legal and political safeguards in a democratizing Europe, the conference looked at two countries, Hungary and Yugoslavia. Péter Paczolay, Professor of Political Theory at the University of Budapest, described the revival in Hungary, after a forty-year absence, of the concept of innate and inviolable rights. These are written into the country's 1989 constitution, in the chapter on basic rights and duties. Two of the new constitutional court's first four cases have dealt with these issues. Rights to life and human dignity are guaranteed, as well as rights to work and social security. Violations of rights are to be judged by an independent judiciary.

Hungarians, disturbed by discriminatory treatment of Hungarian minorities in Romania and Czechoslovakia, see an important task for the forthcoming CSCE summit conference in promoting tolerance for the rights of ethnic groups.

Vojislav Stanovčić, Professor of Political Science at the University of Belgrade, emphasized the difficulties of inculcating the rule of law where a "democratic political culture" and civil society are lacking. He put some hope in the current spread of democratic civilization to eastern Europe, but he pointed out the dearth of democratic tradition in the region except in Czechoslovakia. In this part of Europe law has tended to be regarded as the mere instrument of those in power, rather than as a limitation on that power. It does not provide robust resistance to nationalist passions and yearnings for a strong leader and authoritarian government, or even fascism.

Stanovčić valued the endorsement of the rule of law by the recent CSCE conference in Bonn. He faulted the official Yugoslav concept of rule of law, however, for being confined to implementation of those laws now on the books. Many of these laws are themselves rigid and irrational, he contended, and observance even of the fifty articles dealing with civil rights in the Yugoslav constitution is problematical.

One trial in Bosnia involving Moslem fundamentalists a few years ago, for example, flagrantly violated the precept drawn from Roman law of giving a fair hearing to opposing sides. In it 182 witnesses testified for the prosecutor, while none of the hundred witnesses proposed by the defense was heard. Furthermore, presumption of innocence is violated by inexperienced jurists, and even in such federal laws as one authorizing officials to require a person to prove that all his wealth was earned properly. A new constitutional proposal, similar to provisions in western law, to allow everything that is not expressly forbidden is not widely understood and supported.

In his comments Koenraad Lenaerts, Professor of Law at the University of Leuven and the Belgian judge on the new Court of First Instance of the European Communities, drew on the Hungarian and Yugoslav examples to discuss the CSCE as the meeting place between two philosophies of human rights that diverge over western civil and political individual rights and Soviet social, economic, and cultural rights. He welcomed the setting of some common norms and aspirations at the CSCE Bonn conference as showing that it is now becoming possible to bridge the two views in ways that would have been impossible even ten years ago.

He welcomed as well the applications by Poland, Czechoslovakia, and Hungary to join the Council of Europe and subscribe to the European Convention on Human Rights, which is binding on all Council members. Under this convention individuals (even if they are not citizens) can sue member countries in the European court system for redress of grievances.

The conference adjourned without expressing any formal consensus. But all who participated were inspired by the opportunities for progress beyond the rigidities of the cold war, yet apprehensive concerning the immense political and economic difficulties involved in creating stable democratic governments in eastern Europe.

I. Origins of the New Europe

Chapter 2

The Years 1848 and 1989: The Perils and Profits of Historical Comparisons

Paul W. Schroeder

This is a time for historians to put up or shut up. For years those of us who specialize in international history before 1945 have claimed that understanding today's developments requires the perspective of earlier eras. Confronted now by revolutionary changes in Europe of breathtaking speed and scope, we cannot simply declare that these are new and unprecedented.

Of course they are. One purpose of history is to help distinguish what is really new from what is only apparently so. There is nothing comparable in earlier history to the Helsinki process—no similar international effort under these revolutionary conditions to promote human rights, safeguard peace, and strengthen the international system. The great peace congresses and European Concert conferences of the past are only faintly analogous, if at all. There is also no real historical analogy to the revolutions of 1989. The years 1789 and 1917, which have been suggested, clearly will not do, and 1776 still less.

There is, however, one half-valid analogy, the only serious candidate: 1848. Eighteen forty-eight is famous as the year of failed revolutions—in Trevelyan's phrase, the turning point where history failed to turn. I want briefly to compare 1848 and 1989, not because the 1989 revolutions are headed for the same end—they have certainly not done so thus far—but because some developments in the 1848 revolutions and the decades that followed suggest dangers to be aware of in the 1990s.

Eighteen forty-eight was similar to 1989 in several ways, first in the causes and goals of the movement. The proximate cause was economic, political, and social discontent in the hungry forties; the long-term one was the obsolescence and breakdown of a rigid authoritarian system. The revolutionary goal held in common, though divergently understood, was freedom—economic, political, social, spiritual, and fraternal liberty, an end to the wardship of the state. The course of the revolutions also reminds one of 1989—the speed and ease of their triumph, the confusion and disarray among governments and ruling elites, the rapidity with which positions long rigidly maintained were abandoned, and, at least at first, the minimum of violence required to win great concessions. Nineteen eighty-nine above all reminds one of the spirit of 1848, that springtime of nations with its contagious optimism and seemingly boundless opportunities, the impression that Murphy's Law had been reversed, so that anything that could go right, would. Similar also was an accompanying undertone of fear—fear of counterrevolution, of old authorities and enemies, and, all too soon, of new enemies or rivals in what had seemed a united movement.

The differences between 1989 and 1848, however, are at least as striking. There was more political naivete and utopian expectation in 1848, less awareness of potential problems. The year 1989, in contrast, is remarkable for the general sobriety and skill shown by leaders and followers in the revolutions. The forces of the old order in 1848, more thrown into confusion than overthrown, resorted to force much more quickly—in key instances, within a few months of the revolution's victory. Above all, the lessons learned in the respective revolutions about the use of armed force were exactly opposite. Most governments before 1848 believed that they could not and should not use their armies against their own subjects. They learned in the revolution that they could and should; this more than anything was decisive for its fate. So far, except for China, 1989 has been different (the tension over Lithuania is mounting as this is being written). Governments that formerly used armed force to repress dissent, and justified it, now decline to do so. In 1848–1849 revolutionary coalitions tended to fall apart more quickly and completely than so far in 1989–1990, and governments and ousted leaders were more ready to believe that the old order could be restored and more willing to try to do so.

All this, even if true, serves at best only as an interesting historical footnote and at worst as a distraction, if there is nothing to be learned from the analogy. I think there is something, and will try to bring it out by concentrating on one putatively central point of comparison between 1848 and 1989. The goal, as always in consulting history for purposes of present policy, is not to find a usable past, but if possible to help avoid an unusable future.

The analogy is between the Austrian Empire in 1848 and the Soviet Union in 1989. Before anyone, especially a Soviet representative, protests, let me say that here too the differences probably outweigh the similarities, and the point to be made will concern less how these two powers and their policies compare, and more how outsiders, especially in the West, reacted to their respective revolutions.

To start with the similarities: both powers were at the heart of the respective revolutions. They represented the core and mainstay of the system that was challenged. How they met the challenge, or failed to, would be decisive for the failure or success of revolution elsewhere.

Both faced similar external and internal problems before and during the revolution. Externally: a rigid, outmoded legitimating state ideology; relative economic backwardness; the loss of its empire and/or sphere of influence; and a concomitant disintegration of its previous system of security. Internally: a crying need for modernization to catch up with competitors; a question of whether the regime and its leadership could survive, and beyond that, whether the state itself would hold together when its basic principles were being challenged.

Both states were not merely multinational and multiethnic, but embraced vastly different levels and kinds of culture—religious, social, and political. Both showed a roughly similar slope of development falling from northeast to southeast.

The differences are greater. First, there was no Austrian Gorbachev, or anything like him. No one tried seriously to anticipate major change in Austria and its sphere, much less promote and guide it. The only dynamic revolutionary leader, Kossuth, soon became a rebel; the timid semi-liberal collaborators at Vienna were soon swept away by the military and neo-absolutist counterrevolution.

The Soviet Union today faces the loss of its satellite empire, and with it part of its former security system. But no overt great power threat accompanies this loss, nor is any great rival obviously bent on exploiting Soviet losses. Austria in 1848 faced direct threats from rivals in Germany and Italy, and indirectly from France. At the same time, Austria had a powerful neighbor, Imperial Russia, ready to help it in counterrevolution. The Soviet Union now has nothing similar.

The Soviet Union today, relative to its competitors, is more powerful, more unified, and more modern than Austria was in 1848, with a much larger people forming the central core of the state and a stronger unifying national tradition. The Soviet Union's nationalities problems and revolts are to this point peripheral; Austria's were pervasive and central. Hence in 1848, as often before, there were legitimate grave doubts about the viability and permanence of the Austrian state. There can be, in my view, no serious doubts about the survival of the Soviet state today.

The Soviet Union, to this point, has been far more willing to accept political defeats, adjust to new realities, and continue to promote changes both within its own borders and beyond them than Austria was in 1848–1849. Added to this hopeful note is one demonstrable fact admitting of no controversy: 1989 is not 1848. This is the age of nuclear weapons, of electronic communications, of mass politization and mobilization, of telerevolution.

Again, if this is true, where does it leave us? What is the point?

The point, for me, lies in a disturbingly similar pattern of reactions to the two sets of revolutions. To overstate and oversimplify: in 1848 and after, western leaders and observers, though they knew something of what was happening in Austria and recognized its importance in theory, tended, perhaps because this was beyond their control, to concentrate on what was happening closer to home, especially developments in Germany and Italy which they could marginally influence and for which they might feel a particular sympathy. Thus the West in 1848 and for decades thereafter, without necessarily intending to, tended to act in regard to the problems of Central and eastern Europe as if Austria were no longer a great power, or were not even there. But Austria remained a great power after 1848, though increasingly a marginal one, and it remained indisputably located in the heart of Europe. The combination of western inattention, whether benign or malign, and of Austria's increasingly desperate self-assertion would ultimately prove fatal to old Europe. I fear something similarly tragic and more universally fatal today, if only as a remote possibility. The other observation is directly connected with this. Most textbooks say that the Vienna system, which preserved general peace in Europe after 1815, was destroyed by the 1848 revolutions. This is incorrect. The Vienna system, next to our own the most successful in preserving general peace the world has ever seen, not merely survived the revolutions of 1848, but triumphed over them. Despite revolutions, civil conflicts, and actual interstate wars in 1848–1850 more numerous than can even be stated here, Europe emerged with not one treaty overthrown, not one border changed, and every threatening civil or international war confined and terminated. The period 1848–1850 may be the best example we have of how an international system can control conflict—except perhaps for our current experience. But there is a downside. The Vienna system used itself up in managing the crises of 1848–1850, and collapsed soon thereafter. This is a potential danger in 1990 and after—less, as some fear, that revolutionary changes may directly overthrow the existing international system and lead to war, more that the existing system, in preventing war now, may be used up, become useless for this purpose in the future.

Let me try to put a little flesh on the bare bones of these assertions. What is meant by western inattention to Austria's revolution? Not, certainly, total ignorance or indifference—only the conviction that what happened in Austria itself was important primarily for its effects on the fate of other revolutions in Germany, Italy, and elsewhere. Insofar as westerners paid attention to what happened within Austria, they showed a wide mixture of hostility and sympathy. The desire to see Austria's weakness and distraction continue so that other revolutions could succeed vied with the hope that liberal reformers in Austria would manage to hold onto power for the same end, and for the sake of avoiding a European war. Some hoped that Austria would break up for the sake of national liberation and progress; others hoped that the monarchy would survive and reform. But whatever the prognoses, the key issue for western observers was how this would affect the parts of Europe and/or the general peace, not the fate and health of the monarchy per se.

There was, concomitantly, little recognition of an organic connection between the German and Italian revolutions and the fate of the Habsburg monarchy. The two questions— whether Germany and Italy would be free and united, and whether Austria would survive and solve its internal problems—were somehow seen as separate rather than two sides of the same coin.

There was also relatively little understanding of the impact on the international system of revolution in the monarchy, or even its possible demise, other than the possibility of general war or of shifts in the balance of power; still less of the actual functions and roles played by Austria within the system. No distinction by and large was made, for example, between areas in which Austria's role was now outmoded, superfluous, or harmful (as in holding down Germany and Italy or checking France), and where it remained indispensable and progressive, as in southeastern Europe. No distinction was made between the supposed (and overrated and misunderstood) balance-of-power functions of the monarchy, and its functions as an integrating force in an extremely divided, chaotic, and dangerous portion of Europe.

Most important, what passed in the West for serious consideration of the Austrian problem, i.e., the possibility of Austria's demise or serious weakening and its effects, really consisted of various versions of a common western stance in international affairs: Micawberism, the doctrine of muddling through, hoping that something would turn up. There was Whig-liberal Micawberism, revolutionary Micawberism, realpolitical Micawberism, even conservative Micawberism. In giving Austria useless and sometimes fatuous advice on solving its nationalities problems (as if such problems are ever solved by anyone, are not at best lived with and outlived), or in concocting plans for transforming the empire into a democratic federation or devising a substitute for it—plans which ranged from the earnestly impractical to the downright lunatic—other Europeans could sometimes believe they had done their part to solve the difficulty and preserve world peace.

No predilection for either the Austrian Empire in 1848 or the Soviet Union now is implied by an insistence on the central, indispensable character of each in the international system of its era. It shows no particular love or fascination for the human liver to observe that even if it is unattractive and diseased, before one cuts it out or sees it die one had better know what will replace it or fill its functions in the human body. There was no good substitute in 1848 and after for the existing international system, or for Austria's role within it. We can see that more clearly now. For good or ill, Austria occupied a specific space, a confrontation zone between West and East, modernization and tradition, cultures and religions, and was saddled with its difficulties. In southeastern Europe today, from Transylvania to Albania to Slovenia, one still sees problems which, to be sure, the Austrian Empire did not solve, which it may have made worse—but which its disappearance did not cure either. Something like this holds triply for the Soviet Union. Not only will it remain a superpower and as such a great indispensable factor in world politics for the foreseeable future, it also fulfills specific functions, occupies a particular space, and must deal with a special zone of confrontations and problems where no practical substitute for it can be imagined, much less devised by anyone in the West. In a day of western rejoicing (not to say gloating) over the triumph of economic and political liberalism, it is worth asking whether a laissez-faire Micawberite liberalism in international politics (the usual name for such a policy is "balance of power") has ever worked safely or well, and whether we should risk it now.

Chapter 3

Germany and Europe: Old Dilemmas, New Solutions?

Renata Fritsch-Bournazel

The recent deep changes in East-West relations have clearly shown the importance of a community of culture, memories, and hope in the center of Europe. Revolutionary events have shaken the communist states and produced a world already unrecognizable to those who had accommodated themselves to the political map of a divided continent. The graft of Sovietism in East Central Europe has not taken and, after years of numb changelessness, the legacy of Stalinism has been rejected by the people taking to the streets.

In a year filled with powerful images, none was more dramatic or more hopeful in 1989 than the breaching of the structure that had stood for the harsh division between East and West. When the wall that divided Berlin and sealed an international order crumbled into souvenirs, the cold war system fell apart before the world's eyes. The conservative Christian Democrats' stunning victory in the East German elections of March 18, 1990, an endorsement of Chancellor Kohl's plan for speedy German unity, further accelerates a European upheaval ending the postwar world and beginning something new. Yet, what Europe will become, and how it will do so, is quite unforeseeable.

The end of Stalinist ideology, if not of history, indeed requires a radically new approach to what must again be capitalized as The German Question. The division of the city of Berlin, of Germany, and of the continent came as a result of the war waged by Hitler. At the end of the century, Europe faces a time of promise and surely hopes that there will be a happy ending this time, yet uncertainty prevails about the long-term effects of the continent's new volatility. The formation of a new European peace order will require answering the German question and settling it on terms acceptable both to the Germans and to their neighbors. What Germany and Europe need—and may not get in a world that has acquired simultaneously more freedom and more danger—is a breathing space in which they can weigh their choices.

Mikhail Gorbachev, one of the world's greatest symbols of change, faces the same kind of dilemma. At this point, it remains an unanswerable question whether the Soviet leader is in control of events or events are hurling him forward to an unknown end. He has been breaking up an old bloc to make way for a new Europe, altering the relationship of the Soviet empire with the rest of the world and changing the nature of the empire itself. At the same time one might argue that Gorbachev is not the true progenitor but only the instrument of transformations driven by the forces that are reshaping the world, such as modern media, mounting material aspirations, and consciousness of human rights.

Whereas East Central Europe enters the 1990s in the throes of a continuing anticommunist revolution dominated by the ideals of pluralistic democracy and civil rights, this region-wide triumph for western liberalism paradoxically has left the West in emotional confusion. For the moment, it is apparent that speculation is running ahead of events and that this in itself is adding to uncertainty. At the same time, while western governments compete to reshape Europe and to redefine the proper place of the Germans in the post-Yalta world, they also have to assess how the continent's security needs can be met as the cold war system recedes. The nagging question is about whether Europe, suddenly on the verge of becoming whole and free again, will be able to harmonize the Germans' right to self-determination and the prospects for the reassociation of the two halves of our continent.

Life without the Wall

The construction of the Berlin Wall in August 1961 was a watershed in European and, indeed, international politics. It put a seal on the postwar division of both Germany and the city of

Berlin. It made clear that the Soviet Union was not prepared to stand by as the German Democratic Republic fell apart, and demonstrated the western determination to maintain West Berlin as part of its world. For decades, the Berlin Wall had become the symbol of the cold war. President Ronald Reagan, in his June 1987 speech in West Berlin, cut to the heart of the matter when challenging Gorbachev to tear down the Wall if he wanted to prove his desire for peace and political liberalization. The removal of a scar that has so long defaced Europe, beginning with the opening of the borders on November 9, 1989, was a great day for Berlin, for Germany, and for Europe. The collapse of the Wall also promises the end of political and ideological confrontation in Central Europe beyond the fact that the challenges ahead are at least as daunting as anything the cold war produced.

As the new decade begins, with the prospect of imminent unification, West Germans indeed seek a path out of divisive ideological camps, but the Federal Republic is too deeply rooted in the West to distance itself from its allies. Instead of going at the end of the process of building a new Europe, the Wall has gone at the beginning. Its opening is the key which may help unlock the door to rapid decisions on ending forty-five years of East-West confrontation, formally as well as in fact. The end of the Wall also gives a powerful impetus for new thinking on the future architecture of Europe as a whole.

Blueprints for Reshaping Europe and Germany

From the very beginning, the Federal Republic of Germany has stood on the fault line where three of the postwar world's tectonic plates—East-West relations, the Atlantic alliance, and the European Community (EC)—meet. Konrad Adenauer, the first architect of West German policy and a strong proponent of a western orientation, had built over years an edifice based on what Ralf Dahrendorf once called the "Russian doll principle." alliance with the West meant overcoming past hostilities through Franco-German friendship. This concept fitted neatly into the process of European cooperation and integration and did not contradict the Atlantic alliance, which formed the basis of Germany's security. Western unity and strength, in the long run, would induce the Soviet Union to settle the German question on western terms.

The attractive power of western ideals and values certainly played a role in the dramatic events of 1989, but the real force moving the two Germanies and the two Europes closer together was the mass power of the street, not governments negotiating "from a position of strength" as in the diplomatic blueprints of the 1950s. The Europe of 1992, with its transnational mergers and its commitment to democracy, has indeed become a powerful magnet for the East, and the gloomy mood of "Eurosclerosis" that haunted the minds not long ago seems definitely remote. There is a growing consciousness that the Community needs to be strengthened to confront the challenge of helping the nations of eastern Europe as they move toward greater freedom and to handle the process of German unification.

So far fears that West Germany will be too distracted by the rebuilding of East Germany to continue the building of the European Community have been exaggerated. The EC members will have to accommodate and to manage the political earthquake in East Germany and East Central Europe by providing the two halves of our continent with a model and a vision for the 1990s. To be sure, in the view of Europe's founding fathers, the Community itself was only a stage on the way to the reshaping of Europe as a whole. Yet, not a few West Europeans today secretly wish Warsaw, Budapest, East Berlin, or Prague had postponed their peaceful revolution until after 1992. On the one hand, there is a lot of satisfaction about the westward drift of the Comecon countries, but on the other, the complex task of aiding and eventually integrating the six newly liberated East Central European nations might delay the Economic and Monetary Union, the most ambitious component of the single-market plan.

The fear, particularly widespread in the European Commission and in the capitals of France, Italy, and Belgium, is indeed that an upgrading of the European Community's ties with the emerging democracies of East Central Europe will distract the Community into becoming "wider rather than deeper." The model favored by Jacques Delors, the president of the Community's executive commission, might offer a real chance of reconciling the Europe-building impetus with the new dynamics of the German question: a Europe of "concentric circles," of which the democratic, industrialized West would form the core. The neutrals and the former communist states would figure as EC satellites until they are prepared to take on the political and economic responsibility of Community membership, with the only exception of East Germany that is offered a fast track. Eventually, the challenge of promoting German unification under a European roof will foster the political will that is needed to create the United States of Europe—the dream of the postwar generation.

The Russian Question

The German question, to be sure, weighs heavily on the prospects for the reassociation of the two halves of Europe. The emerging new order of a Europe stretching from Brest to Brest is bound to affect the Germans' role in the world. Germany, however defined, will at once become the very heart of the European continent, linking instead of dividing East and West. As to the Soviet Union, the shape in which it will ultimately emerge from the present turmoil remains totally unpredictable. As the reverberations of the revolutions on its borders swell back into the Soviet republics, Mikhail Gorbachev may well find himself confronted with decisions as dramatic as those that faced East Central European leaders in 1989. The demise of orthodox communism in East Germany and in East Central Europe is a positive boon to the Soviet leader in his ideological battles at home with communist conservatives. Now he faces another challenge: to allow Soviet citizens the freedoms being won by others in 1989, as the democratic revolution and the thirst for freedom have spread like an uncontainable epidemic.

The Soviet crisis on top of the German question is seen as a potentially explosive mixture by many West Europeans whose optimism about prospects for almost boundless change in the East has started to shrivel. This new pessimism conveys a different meaning to the debate about the Gorbachev challenge that during the past focussed on the alternative "to help or not to help." Now that the "Genscher line" (we must help Gorbachev out of our own interest in his success) seems to have become the majority view in the West, the new Russian question to be answered by the West is how the Soviet Union fits into the new Europe. To the extent that he has any bargaining power left, Gorbachev will want something in return for giving up military and economic dominance in East Central Europe and for his not standing in the way of German unity.

Under Gorbachev the limits of Soviet tolerance have indeed become blurred. It will no longer be the military function of the Atlantic alliance to maintain the political status quo, and there is a serious danger of its losing purpose and coherence. The complex and delicate task of managing change will be the top item on the agenda of the 1990s, together with the preparation of mutual security and overall stability, while the turbulence of political change settles down into a new European order.

The Germany and the Europe We Deserve

Changing the Germans by means of rapprochement and the promise of equal treatment in future were the two principles on which advocates of Franco-German reconciliation like Joseph Rovan and Alfred Grosser based their attitudes after the end of the Second World War. Now that we are facing once again the problem of balancing German national aspirations against the claims of European stability, it might be useful to remember their postwar reflections on "the Germany we deserve" and on the "coresponsibility for the German future."

Both the Americans and the Soviets, as well as the neighbors, have gone a long way to accommodate West German wishes and interests in the process of German unification. Many countries have a lot at stake in the terms by which this great event is accomplished, and four—Britain, France, the Soviet Union, and the United States—have legal rights going back to World War II. The Germans have a right to self-determination, but like all rights, it is accompanied by responsibilities—among others, to Germany's neighbors. Their ability to provide guarantees and reassurances, particularly about the inviolability of borders, will influence the character of Europe well into the next century.

Charles de Gaulle, speaking at a press conference on March 25, 1959, envisioned the future of Germany as follows:

> Reunification of the two segments into a single Germany that would be entirely free seems to us to be the normal destiny of the German people, provided that the German people did not call its present borders into question, east

and west, north and south; and that it tended toward integration one day in a contractual organization of all Europe for cooperation, freedom, and peace.

A new generation of European political institutions is now beginning to take shape, still unclear in its form but momentous in its implications. The only existing forum that includes both eastern and western Europe, as well as the United States, Canada, and the Soviet Union, the Conference on Security and Cooperation in Europe, probably will be used as the medium for both arms control negotiations and debate over Europe's new architecture as well as about Germany's future place in it.

Tomorrow's Europe will be greatly influenced by what happens in Germany, and by other countries' feelings about it. It is the responsibility of the neighbors not to apply a double standard to the entire German nation because of the past, and it is the responsibility of the Germans to show Europe and the world that there is nothing to fear. This was Czechoslovak President Václav Havel's advice to his countrymen during West German President Richard von Weizsäcker's visit to Prague in March 1990, which was arranged to coincide with the 51st anniversary of Hitler's arrival in the city at the head of an occupying army.

Chapter 4

The European Neutrals Face the 1990s

Joseph Kruzel

The neutrals and nonaligned states are not at the center of the story as the geopolitical map of Europe is redrawn. They are on the periphery, affected by the political, economic, and military forces sweeping the continent but not themselves the primary agents of change. The Euroneutrals are profoundly influenced by the waning of Soviet power and the collapse of the Warsaw Pact, the democratization of eastern Europe, and the reunification of Germany, but these events are essentially beyond their control.

Despite their marginal role, it is worth examining the neutral and nonaligned countries not only because their citizens are a significant percentage of the residents of the new European home but also because their basic assumptions of foreign policy are called into question by the forces transforming Europe.

Two problems face the European neutrals. The first is a conceptual challenge following from the diminished sense of threat in East-West relations. The second challenge is economic, and derives from the European Community's (EC) commitment to a single barrier-free market in 1992 and to further political integration beyond that date. These two issues raise important questions about what it means to be neutral in an international system quite unlike the one that gave rise to neutrality in the first place.

The Conceptual Challenge

Bipolarity has been the dominant feature of international politics and the basic determinant of contemporary neutrality in the post–World War II era. The neutrals have stayed outside the system of competing military alliances and have set as their primary objective to remain disentangled from the East-West conflicts.

Many neutrality proponents have advanced a concept of active neutrality that would lead the world out of the quagmire of war-fixated bipolar international politics. This vision, dismissed not long ago by realists as idealistic fantasy, now seems an accurate assessment of the direction in which Europe is headed (although inspired less by the neutrals' example than by the collapse of communism). In so radically altered an international system the Euroneutrals must ask themselves what is left of the concept of neutrality. What does neutrality mean when the confrontation that defined it begins to fade away? Without two blocs to be between, what is there to be neutral about?

In the early 1990s it was difficult to imagine a return to a more hostile and threatening Soviet security policy, but any pronouncement on the death of East-West tensions was still premature. If anything is more dangerous than a cohesive and expanding empire it is a disintegrating and contracting one, and the rumble of tanks through Vilnius in the spring of 1990 served as a pointed reminder that military force was still a live option. Empires do not often collapse in a stable and peaceful manner.[1]

Even if East-West tensions faded away entirely, the decline of Soviet power and influence could lead to the emergence of conflicts held in check for decades by an assertive Soviet state. Border disputes between Germany and Poland, resentment in Hungary over Romania's treatment of Transylvanian Hungarians, Czech and Slovak differences over power-sharing in the federal government, Slovenia's threatened secession from Yugoslavia—these and other issues could lead to the reemergence of contending coalitions that would make a tradition of neutrality a valuable foreign policy resource. The Conference on Security and Cooperation in Europe (CSCE) may someday become an effective pan-European collective security organization, but until a new structure of European security is firmly established, the neutrals would do well to hold to their traditional security postures and policies.

If the millennium comes, the Euroneutrals will have to make some adjustments in declaratory policy but relatively few changes in military force posture. Certainly their force structures and doctrines will require less revision than those of the North Atlantic Treaty Organization (NATO) and (former) Warsaw Pact countries. With some rewriting of white papers and defense plans, what served the neutrals well in the cold war will provide a sound basis for defense planning in the post–cold war era.[2]

During the cold war most Euroneutrals assumed that their only real security threat was the threat of being caught up in a conflict between the two military alliances. They eschewed any notion of regional rivalry, irredentism, or other grievance with neighboring states that might lead to armed conflict.[3] The task of defense was to make an attack by either alliance not worth the cost in terms of time lost, manpower and equipment expended, and opportunity sacrificed by engagement with a peripheral actor. The neutrals hoped to make themselves so difficult to conquer and cumbersome to occupy that Warsaw Pact and NATO military planners would choose to fight World War III somewhere else.

The Euroneutrals are subject to the same economic and demographic problems facing other European states, but they already spend less on defense in per-capita terms than their NATO and Warsaw Pact neighbors, and their go-it-alone defense posture means that they are not embroiled in the "burden-shedding" arguments that cause such intra-alliance friction in NATO. Moreover, their basic defense posture holds up well in a less threatening but also less certain strategic environment. In the cold war the threat was to avoid getting caught up in an East-West conflict and the objective was to demonstrate to adversaries that it was more cost-effective to bypass than invade. In the post-cold war era the threat is less evident, but the objective is the same: to maintain a force posture sufficient to make the cost-benefit assessment of attack negative for any potential aggressor.

The real challenge posed to the Euroneutrals by the changing strategic landscape of Europe is not in military force posture itself, but in the effect that the new security picture will have on the very conception of neutrality. In this regard the four major Euroneutrals divide into two groups. On the one hand are Switzerland and Sweden, states with long traditions of neutrality predating the cold war; on the other hand are Finland and Austria, "losers" in World War II whose neutrality was forced upon them by geostrategic necessity and the victorious powers.

Austria's existence as an independent, nonoccupied state is the result of its acceptance of neutrality. The same is true, in a less direct sense, for Finland. As creatures of the cold war, Austria and Finland will be more affected by the waning of cold war tensions than other Euroneutrals. Their autonomy has been the result of a commitment to remain apart from bloc politics. With fewer issues being defined in bloc-to-bloc terms, neutrality will no longer offer so clear a guiding light in Austrian and Finnish foreign policy.

Gorbachev used the occasion of his 1989 state visit to Finland to repudiate the Brezhnev doctrine and declare that the Soviet Union has no moral or political right to intervene in the affairs of its neighbors. Finland, Gorbachev said, "is a model of relations between a big country and a small country, a model of relations between states with different social systems, a model of relations between neighbors."[4] Gorbachev's recognition of "neutral Finland" was the first time a Soviet leader had explicitly acknowledged Finland's status as a neutral state and was taken by the Finns as repudiation of Moscow's claim that Finland must maintain a special relationship with the Soviet Union. Switzerland and Sweden, by contrast with Austria and Finland, were well established as neutrals before World War II (and were well served in that conflict by their posture of neutrality). Theirs is an organic neutrality, developed from the collective experience of centuries, not something imposed by the cold war and thus less influenced by its passing.

All the European neutrals, old and new, will be less constrained by the need to meet external expectations about neutrality. They will be able to establish foreign policy agendas with less worry about the credibility of neutrality policy. The Euroneutrals will become more "ordinary," and their relations with other states will be more influenced by geostrategic and economic considerations than by the dictates of neutrality. Finnish-Soviet and Austrian-German relations may come more closely to resemble relations between other small and large states—Canada and the United States, for example—than special cases created by the obligations of neutrality.

Even if cold war tensions were to disappear entirely, some neutral states would enjoy residual benefits from maintaining their traditional posture. Ireland's neutrality has been more a way of distancing the country from Great Britain than a response to the cold war. Since it was never much affected by the East-West conflict, Irish neutrality will not be much influenced by its passing. For Austria, and perhaps for Switzerland as well, neutrality will continue to offer some protection against a unified German state whose *volk* might be construed to include citizens of those two states. Without communism East Germany quickly lost its rationale for independent existence; with neutrality Austria and Switzerland will have a means of defining and distinguishing themselves from their larger neighbor.

If the passing of the cold war frees the Euroneutrals from some foreign policy limitations imposed by neutrality, it also restricts opportunities they enjoyed during times of heightened East-West hostility. In the neutrals' view, the rigid alliance structure and ensuing problems of communication between the blocs created an opportunity for the neutrals to mediate, build bridges, and offer technical services to the international community, especially the two military blocs. Whether Washington and Moscow really needed interlocutors in Stockholm or Vienna is a question for debate, but the neutrals did provide many important international services—the Red Cross, venues for numerous conferences and negotiations, and a valuable intermediary function in CSCE. In return the neutrals gained important international visibility, far more than allied countries of comparable size, and an opportunity to reinforce their neutral image. In the post–cold war era such functions appear less important, both for the neutrals themselves and for the other states in the international system.

Neutrality gave states holding to the posture an opportunity to enter new arenas and play a far more active and visible role on the world scene than other states of comparable size. Olaf Palme and Bruno Kreisky embodied this concept of activist neutrality. In the post–cold war era the neutrals, like other small states, may occasionally produce an extraordinary leader, but they will lose the special status they claimed for having a view of international relations uncorrupted by the biases of aligned states.

The Economic Challenge

Since its earliest formulation by David Mitrany and Jean Monnet, the European Community has had the ultimate objective of politically integrating the sovereign states of Europe. Because this goal was incompatible with legal neutrality, the European neutrals sought some means of association with the Community other than full membership. Through the European Free Trade Association (EFTA) and other mechanisms the Euroneutrals were able to preserve their neutrality and enjoy the benefits of economic prosperity at the same time. And while the European Community paid lip service to the idea of eventual political integration, it made little progress toward the sort of union that would create problems for the Euroneutrals. This comfortable *modus vivendi* is now threatened by the Single European Act creating a single barrier-free market by 1992 and the European Community's commitment to an eventual monetary union.

The question for 1992 and beyond is whether the neutrals will continue to remain outside, faithful to the principles of neutrality but marginal actors in the new Europe, or enter the new European home, take a seat at the table, transcend nationalism, and adjust neutrality to the requirements of a new international order.

In practical terms the choice is not quite between these two extremes, for no Euroneutral seriously contemplates going it alone in the new Europe. Ireland has long been a member of the European Community, and all of the others have recognized and accepted the imperatives of economic competitiveness, liberal trade policies, and open markets. Many large corporations in neutral states have merged or signed partnerships with businesses within the European Community, so industrially the Euroneutrals are *de facto* members of the Community even if they stand *de jure* outside its political structure. The "Communitization" of the neutrals has already forced the neutrals to adopt the rules and regulations of the European Community as their own simply to ensure that their products are acceptable when they are exported to the Community.

The real range of choice is between membership with reservations and conditions offering some safeguards for neutrality, or some associate status preserving neutrality but allowing participation in the economic activities of the Community. The irony is that preserving neutrality and remaining outside the European Community would effectively deny the neutrals a role in EC decision-making without in any way reducing their need to conform to EC decisions.

For the short term (that is, until after 1992) the question of membership has been set aside by an EC-EFTA agreement to establish a new "European Economic Space" (EES) joining member states of the two organizations in a free trade zone. This solution offers the Euroneutrals (as well as Iceland and Norway, the other EFTA members) a reprieve: participation in the new European single market without formal membership in the Community and without having to deal with the implications for deeper political integration. There is even discussion about devising an EES forum that will allow EFTA members some influence over Community decisions.

Whether the plan for European Economic Space is a stopgap measure or the basis for a long-term solution remains to be seen. If the citizens of neutral states see the choice as between economic growth or unfettered neutrality, it is questionable how much sacrifice they will make to preserve the principle of neutrality. When cold war tensions were high, neutrality and independence were not such artificial abstractions, but in the post–cold war era the value of neutrality may seem marginal or even negative. When neutrality is perceived as a liability rather than an asset, all sorts of economic and political trade-offs will have to be recalculated. Euroneutral governments are already feeling pressure from business leaders to apply for EC membership and leave the problem of adjusting neutrality to Foreign Ministry lawyers. Even Switzerland has changed its tune, no longer ruling out "forever" the possibility of EC membership.

The deeper question posed by the Single European Act is what neutrality really means in an increasingly interdependent European and world economy, whatever a state's formal relationship with the European Community. In monetary policy Austria already follows the lead of the German *Bundesbank*, and over two-thirds of its trade is with EC countries. Like it or not, Austria and the other Euroneutrals have become dependent on the European Community.

Neutrality in the Post–Cold War Era

In its earliest conception neutrality meant not taking sides in an armed conflict involving other states. No state was permanently neutral, all states were occasionally neutral, and most states were neutral most of the time. A neutral enjoyed certain rights and assumed certain obligations during a war, but when conflict ended, so did the commitment to neutrality. Neutrality was not so much a principle as an expedient. It was a strategy for small-state survival in the anarchy of international relations, an option for small states desiring not to be caught up in the quarrels of large states or alliance systems.

Historically, the European neutrals have been torn between the go-it-alone isolationism implied by neutrality and a desire to join in collective efforts to enhance international order and reduce the risk of war. In theory, neutrality and collective security are mutually exclusive concepts; more of one should mean less of the other. But diplomacy has a way of triumphing over logic, and the European neutrals have generally managed to combine a strong sense of nationalism with a commitment to participation in the affairs of the global community. All European states with neutralist tendencies joined the League of Nations and, with the exception of Switzerland, accepted without reservation its commitment to sanctions. All the Euroneutrals except Switzerland joined the United Nations, and have played an active role in the organization since its inception.

Joining with other European states in some loose and inclusive supranational political order can thus be seen as consistent with previous efforts at collective action. And despite uneasiness at being seen as models, two Euroneutrals have national experience that could serve as forerunners of a new Europe. The loose confederation of the Habsburgs is one example; another is Switzerland, whose political institutions have managed to accommodate diverse cultures, languages, and religions into a miniature version of the new European home.

In one sense the problem facing the neutrals in an integrated Europe is simply a variant of the problem confronting all states: how to preserve the unique and distinctive elements of national identity within a confederated European Community. Neutrality is only one such element, and perhaps not the most difficult to reconcile. For the Swiss, the political system of direct democracy through referenda may be as great an obstacle to EC membership as a commitment to neutrality. For the Austrians, liberalizing a largely corporatist economy, adjusting the social partnership of labor and industry, and protecting farmers from a flood of cheaper agricultural products will pose problems as nettlesome as negotiating safeguards for neutrality. But in another very important way, neutrality poses a special problem not faced by states already tied to the political, economic, and military structures of western Europe.

Writing in 1939, Hans Morgenthau argued that neutrality was essentially a consequence of balance-of-power politics, and that the replacement of the balance of power by a hegemonic relationship among the European nations would necessarily endanger neutrality.[5] A half-century later the replacement of bloc politics by a functionally integrated European Community will present neutrality with another major challenge.

Neutrality has never been an end in itself. It has always been a means to an end, the end being preservation of national independence and autonomy. But in the new Europe absolute sovereignty will be impossible to achieve and undesirable even if feasible. When the goal of foreign policy changes, the means must be adjusted accordingly.

It may be that neutrality cannot survive the transition. If the importance of the nation-state in European politics continues to fade, so too may neutrality lose its motivating spirit. Someday neutrality may be remembered as an artifact of an outmoded and dangerous international system that admitted no higher authority than the nation-state.

Such a day, if it ever comes, is a long way off. Over the centuries neutrality has adjusted to very different types of international system—the classical balance of power in the nineteenth century, the collective security system of the interwar period, the bipolarity of the cold war. Of these three arrangements only the balance of power was theoretically conducive to neutrality, yet the policy has endured.

The new European home will likely have an inventive if complicated design that will accommodate European states in various configurations to deal with a variety of issues. Europe will be integrated with a bewildering array of cross-cutting associations: NATO, WEU, EC, EFTA, CSCE, and others yet to be created. Within this acronymic maze the neutrals may be able to preserve their neutrality while participating in most affairs of the new order. If so, it will be a new concept of neutrality. There is no going back to the old model—rigid, isolationist, insular, and autarchic—because the conditions that gave rise to that concept of neutrality are fading away. Classical neutrality assumed anarchy and the threat of war as fundamental conditions of international politics. If anarchy yields to supranational order and the risk of war continues to decline, the European neutrals will be forced to rethink and perhaps reinvent a concept that has proven its versatility and flexibility over centuries of use.

Notes

[1]Paul Kennedy, *The Rise and Fall of the Great Powers* (New York: Random House, 1987), p. 514.

[2]Kruzel, "The European Neutrals, National Defense, and International Security," *Comparative Strategy,* Vol. 8:3, Spring 1989, pp. 1-19.

[3]The important and conspicuous exceptions are Albania/Yugoslavia and Ireland.

[4]Bill Keller, "Gorbachev, in Finland, Disavows Any Right of Regional Intervention," *New York Times*, October 26, 1989, p. 1.

[5]Hans Morgenthau, "The Resurrection of Neutrality in Europe," *American Political Science Review*, Vol. 33 (1939), p. 482.

Chapter 5

Democratization and Change in Eastern Europe

F. Stephen Larrabee

Eastern Europe is today in the midst of the most dramatic period of change since the end of World War II. The changes taking place are likely to reshape dramatically the map of Europe and the postwar security order based on the existence of two mutually antagonistic blocs. The collapse of communism in eastern Europe has shattered the old security order. The West is now faced with the task of constructing a new security order out of the wreckage of the old bipolar system which is rapidly crumbling.

This new security order will be neither stable nor long enduring, however, unless eastern Europe is firmly integrated into it. Indeed, assisting the stable transition to democracy in eastern Europe will be one of the major challenges facing the West in the 1990s. A failure to meet this challenge successfully could have major repercussions for European stability over the next decade as well as for the process of western integration itself.

The transition to democracy in eastern Europe is likely to be bumpy and uneven. It will be complicated by four factors in particular:

The "dual nature" of the transition. The countries of eastern Europe will have to undergo a dual transition: to change radically *both* their political and economic systems simultaneously. This differentiates the situation in eastern Europe from that in western Europe and Latin America, where successful transitions from authoritarian to democratic rule have been undertaken. The countries of western Europe emerged from World

War II with their economies destroyed. However, the basic managerial talent and know-how needed to run the economies remained. They simply had to be mobilized and properly utilized.

This is not the case in eastern Europe. The countries of this region will have to carry out political change and economic change in tandem. This is likely to put an enormous burden on many of these countries, and significantly complicate the process of democratization. The risks of "system breakdown" are thus quite high.

Rising popular expectations. Popular expectations in eastern Europe today are high and in many cases unrealistic. There is a general expectation that now, after communism has collapsed, life will improve significantly. Moreover, after years of deprivation the populations are tired of empty promises and waiting. They want prosperity—*now*! (This feeling is particularly strong in the German Democratic Republic, and is one of the driving forces behind the more vocal calls for reunification since last November.) Given the poor performance of their economies, the democratizing regimes of eastern Europe will be hard pressed to satisfy these expectations. Any economic improvement is likely to be slow and gradual. Indeed, in the short run things are likely to get worse, not better.

The gap between rising popular expectations and declining living standards will pose a severe test for fragile democratic governments with little experience in dealing with the vagaries of the market. Authoritarian governments can institute wage and price restraints or cut back on consumer demand relatively easily through repression (Ceausescu's Romania provides a good example). Democratic or democratizing regimes, however, must be sensitive to the demands of their populations. Therein lies the central paradox: satisfying these demands for immediate gratification may undercut the prospects for long-term recovery; failure to satisfy these demands, however, may erode support for the regime and lead to growing social unrest and political instability.

Lack of democratic traditions and experience. With the exception of Czechoslovakia, none of the East European countries has any lengthy experience with democracy. For a good part of the interwar period Hungary, Poland, Romania, and Bulgaria were under authoritarian rule of one sort or another. The democratic institutions that existed before World War II were largely destroyed by the communists. Thus for most of these countries the process of institution-building and political modernization will not be easy.

Minority problems. With the exception of Poland, all the countries in eastern Europe have significant minorities on their territory, many of which have long-standing grievances against the ruling majority. Communist rule and Soviet domination suppressed these problems, but did not resolve them. As Soviet control loosens and the democratization process proceeds, many of these nationality problems are likely to come bubbling to the surface again in more assertive forms. *Glasnost'* will intensify this problem—as the Soviet experience illustrates—since the disaffected minorities will be freer to express their grievances. At the same time weak, insecure governments may try to deflect attention from their internal problems by "playing the nationalist card."

Overall, what we are likely to witness is an "eastern Europe of multiple speeds," with some countries, like Czechoslovakia, making the transition relatively smoothly and others, like Romania and Bulgaria, having much more difficulty and taking longer. Indeed, it may no longer be useful—if, in fact, it ever was—to use the term "eastern Europe." Eastern Europe was an artificial concept which reflected the political division of Europe into two blocs that emerged at the end of World War II, one headed by the United States, the other by the Soviet Union. Prior to that Hungary, Poland, and Czechoslovakia had been considered a part of "Central Europe" and they saw themselves culturally, geographically, and historically as part of Europe. In contrast, Romania and Bulgaria had been viewed as part of the Balkans and were not considered an integral part of Europe proper.

In the coming decade this historical differentiation is likely to reassert itself. With a little luck, and notwithstanding some initial difficulties and setbacks, Hungary, Poland, and Czechoslovakia are likely to make the transition to democracy and again become a part of Europe, establishing close ties with the European Community (EC) and other western institutions like the Council of Europe. Eventually all three may even become members of the European Community or at least attain a special association with it.

The process of democratization in the Balkans, however, will probably be more problematic. Romania, Bulgaria, and

Yugoslavia are likely to be characterized by a significant degree of political instability and fragmentation. Indeed, Yugoslavia could cease to be an integral state. But even if Yugoslavia remains united, Croatia and Slovenia are likely to expand ties to Central Europe—Austria, Hungary, and Czechoslovakia—while Serbia, Macedonia, and Bosnia-Herzegovina will seek closer ties to their Balkan neighbors, and we are likely to witness an increase in Balkan regional cooperation, at least on the economic level.

Any attempt by Serbia, however, to impose a highly centralized system on Yugoslavia (which it would inevitably dominate) will be strongly resisted by Croatia and Slovenia and could lead to greater pressure for secession by those republics and even to civil war. Indeed, over the next decade ethnic nationalism and secessionist pressures in Yugoslavia are likely to pose the greatest threat to security and stability in Europe. Unfortunately, the dangers raised by these pressures have largely been overshadowed by developments elsewhere in eastern Europe and disintegrative tendencies in the Soviet Union. However, if these trends are not arrested, the Balkans could again become the "powder keg of Europe."

The Economic Dimension

The Soviet role in eastern Europe in the next decade will be radically diminished in comparison with what it has been over the past four decades. The two main instruments for maintaining Soviet control in eastern Europe—the Council for Mutual Economic Assistance (Comecon) and the Warsaw Pact—are in advanced states of decomposition. Both are likely to be restructured and gradually disbanded or allowed to atrophy. In the interim, however, both will probably be maintained—albeit in radically altered form—as the East European countries try to decide whether to maintain them or abolish them completely.

In the case of Comecon there are significant obstacles to immediate dismantlement. The countries of eastern Europe conduct between 40 and 80 percent of their trade within Comecon. If Comecon were to be disbanded, they would have to redirect their trade to third markets. This would be very difficult and costly. Moreover, the East European member countries are highly dependent on Soviet energy supplies which they obtain at below world market prices. Thus in the medium term Comecon will probably be kept alive, at least as a mechanism for regulating bilateral relations, as the East European countries attempt to restructure their economies along market lines and gradually reorient their trade.

The first steps in this direction were taken at the 46th Comecon session in Sofia in December 1989. At this meeting the member-states agreed to begin trading in hard currency in 1991. However, there is considerable dissatisfaction with the idea among the East European members. The reform works to the advantage of the Soviet Union since Moscow is an energy exporter, while the East European countries largely export substandard manufactured goods which are not competitive in the world market. At present the East European countries receive energy from the USSR at below market prices and pay in soft currency. An immediate switch to hard currency would be devastating to the East European members, which do not have the means to expand export earnings quickly to cover the increased costs of imported energy. Eastern Europe would run a large trade deficit with the Soviet Union and would suffer a drop in its purchasing power vis-à-vis the Soviet Union of close to 30 percent. Thus some way will have to be found to ease the transition, either by Moscow allowing a grace period in which the deficit is written off as aid, or by obtaining western credits or assistance.

Nonetheless, the East European member-states seem determined to proceed with a radical restructuring of Comecon. At a meeting of experts in March it was recommended that two of the organization's most important and unpopular functions—multilateral cooperation and coordination—should be abolished. The importance of the Secretariat, traditionally headed by a Soviet official, was also downgraded. In the future, the Secretariat will become an information center similar to the Organization for Economic Cooperation and Development (OECD). These decisions and recommendations will be submitted to ministers for approval at a meeting in May which will prepare the way for a full-scale summit of East European leaders to be held in the summer of 1990.

The stagnation of Comecon has sparked a search for alternatives. One concept that has found new currency is subregional cooperation. Proposals for establishing a Central European Economic Federation composed of Czechoslovakia,

Poland, and Hungary are being discussed. Hungary has also shown strong interest in the Alpen-Adria regional cooperation project, and in November the foreign ministers of Hungary, Italy, Yugoslavia, and Austria met in Budapest to discuss co-operation along these lines. Poland has also expressed interest in a federation with Czechoslovakia. However, Czechoslovak Foreign Minister Jiri Dienstbier has expressed reservations about the idea, noting that what was needed was not new forms of closed integration but an opening up of the eastern economies to the world market.

Rather than revising Comecon or relying on other regional organizations, most leaders in eastern Europe see ties to an increasingly dynamic and prosperous European Community as the best hope for resolving their serious economic problems over the long run. Poland, Hungary, and Czechoslovakia have all signed new liberalized trade agreements with the European Community. Hungary has also stated that it would like to obtain full EC membership, though it recognizes this probably cannot occur for at least a decade.

This strong East European interest in the European Community poses new dilemmas for the Community and makes some rethinking of its role necessary. In particular, it raises the question of whether the European Community should give priority to "deepening" the process of integration to include issues of security or whether it should concentrate on "broadening" its role and integrating eastern Europe (or parts of it) into its ranks in some form. While the processes are not totally mutually exclusive, concentrating on one would have implications for the other. A concentration on "deepening" the European Community and expanding its role in security issues would make any association of the East European countries problematic, since the Soviet Union would object to their joining a western organization that had a strong military component. A concentration on "broadening" the European Community, however, risks slowing the momentum toward integration and diluting the Community's unity and sense of purpose. In short, the difficulties of absorbing underdeveloped countries like Greece, Spain, and Portugal would be reinforced by the additional problems of trying to integrate weak command economies into the process of transition.

The Delors concept of a "Europe of multiple speeds" in which there are several "concentric circles" or zones of integration may provide a solution to at least some of these dilemmas. The first zone would be composed of the original six members of the European Community plus any others willing to commit themselves to far-reaching political, military, and economic integration. This zone would be complemented by several other zones, requiring a lesser degree of transfer of sovereignty and integration. Such an arrangement would provide a framework for accommodating change in the East while not holding up the pace of western integration.

Some observers have suggested that rather than seeking association with the European Community, the countries of eastern Europe ought to join the European Free Trade Association (EFTA). There are two problems with this suggestion, however. First, the East Europeans do not want to go this route. At best, they see EFTA as a way station on the road to Brussels. Second, the EFTA countries reject the proposal. The six members of EFTA are looking toward negotiations with the European Community. They believe that EFTA can only preserve its identity and participate in the Single European Market if it is composed of very rich, competitive, and stable countries with a long history of cooperation. This cannot be done if EFTA is forced to absorb its poorer cousins from eastern Europe. Thus, on closer examination, the "EFTA option" looks increasingly like a nonstarter.

The Security Dimension

The rapid changes in eastern Europe have dramatically altered the European security order. Bluntly put, the Warsaw Pact is in a process of rapid decomposition. With the changes in eastern Europe, the ideological rationale for the pact has disappeared. If the Vienna negotiations on Conventional Forces in Europe (CFE) succeed, much of the military rationale will be eliminated as well. Few East Europeans currently perceive much of a threat from the West. Fewer still will feel a threat after a CFE agreement.

Moreover, the Soviet Union may be forced out of eastern Europe unilaterally, with or without a CFE agreement. Czechoslovakia and Hungary are currently negotiating with Moscow to withdraw all Soviet troops from their soil by the end of 1991. As the "two plus four" talks proceed, pressures will also grow for a significant reduction—and eventually the elimination—of Soviet troops in the German Democratic Republic. (There are no Soviet troops stationed in Romania or Bulgaria. Thus the Soviets at least will be spared the humiliation of these two allies joining the open chorus of "Russians go home.")

In addition, the East Europeans have begun to make a number of unilateral cuts in their own military forces and reduce conscription time. In 1989 Poland reduced its troops by 33,000 men and another 10,000 are scheduled to be cut in 1990. The term of military conscription in Poland has been reduced from 24 months to 18 months. Czechoslovakia has announced it will also cut the length of mandatory service from 24 months to 18 months. Hungary has shortened conscription time from 18 to 12 months, and will cut 27,500 troops from its force this year. Together with the 9,300-man reduction made this year, this means that the Hungarian military will be 35 percent smaller.

German unification, moreover, will remove the most important military member of the Warsaw Pact, accelerating the alliance's decomposition. Even if German unification is delayed, the value of East Germany as a member of the pact has been reduced to almost zero. The East German army has virtually disintegrated. New recruits are no longer showing up for exercises, while many officers are seeking employment in the West German Bundeswehr.

As a result of these developments, the Warsaw Pact has become an increasingly hollow shell. It is likely to be dissolved in the near future or transformed into a loose, nonbinding mechanism for consultation and coordination of foreign and arms control policy. At the same time, the current bilateral treaties between the Soviet Union and the other Warsaw Pact member-states will probably be renegotiated in order to put relations on a more equal footing. Some countries, notably Poland, may wish to keep some Soviet troops stationed on their soil as a hedge against a powerful reunited Germany. Most, however, will want all Soviet troops out.

These changes will inevitably have an impact on western security needs and make some rethinking of the North Atlantic Treaty Organization's (NATO) role necessary. As NATO concentrates more on political functions in the future, some aspects of European defense may be able to be assumed by a strengthened Western European Union. Indeed, the changes in eastern Europe are likely to give new impetus to the debate about strengthening the "European pillar" of NATO and to a search for new alternatives, including the establishment of an independent European Defense Community, separate from but loosely linked to the United States and/or NATO.

More attention will also have to be paid to the role of all-European security structures in preserving stability in Europe. Conceivably some security functions could gradually be assumed by an all-European Security Council composed of select members of both alliances, including the two superpowers, as well as some neutral and nonaligned countries. Expanding the all-European dimensions of the current Conference on Security and Cooperation in Europe structure while transforming NATO in a more political direction would also help to defuse Soviet and East European fears of a united Germany. Germany would be constrained both by its ties to NATO as well as by integration into an expanded all-European security system of which the USSR and the countries of eastern Europe would be an integral part.

The changes in eastern Europe also will require some rethinking of the current approach to conventional arms control. As a result of these changes, the CFE framework, which is based on a bloc-to-bloc approach, is becoming obsolete. The current ceilings, moreover, could legitimize higher Soviet troop levels than the Soviet Union might otherwise be allowed to keep in Central Europe. Thus once CFE I is completed, a new negotiating framework will need to be devised. It may still be useful to keep the "23" (or 22, if France refuses to participate) framework to negotiate many conventional arms control issues, but only on the understanding that the East European countries participate on an "individual basis" and not as a bloc with imposed consensus.

The "two plus four" talks are also likely to affect CFE. Many of the CFE's key issues, such as troop reductions and nuclear weapons, will also be discussed in the talks on German unification. Indeed, it is likely that these talks, which will precede the initiation of CFE II, may provide a framework for subsequent negotiations.

Chapter 6

The Diplomacy of Europe Whole and Free

James E. Goodby

It is an unlikely midwife to a new Europe, this process which most Americans have never heard of and which has no name worth remembering. The specialists call it the Conference on Security and Cooperation in Europe (CSCE), or the Helsinki process, and refer to its founding charter as the Helsinki Final Act. Better known are the human rights organizations associated with this process—Helsinki Watch and Helsinki Commission. Ignored in the United States through most of its 15-year history, the Conference on Security and Cooperation in Europe has emerged as a facilitator and safety net, an instrument which bridges the past and the future, and which provides the inspiration for a new European concert system whose outlines already can be dimly perceived. Later this year, very likely, a summit meeting of the 35 European and North American CSCE participants will begin to build a structure that Secretary of State Baker has called "the new European security system."

Mikhail Gorbachev helped to define the current European agenda. His concept of a "common European home" struck a responsive chord in all of Europe, East and West, just as de Gaulle's vision of a "Europe from the Atlantic to the Urals" caught the imagination of an earlier generation of Europeans. George Bush has spoken of a "Europe whole and free" and in

This paper was originally prepared as a lecture and was presented by the author at the National War College, Washington, D.C., April 5, 1990.

so doing underscored the values which gave the idea of united Europe such emotional appeal. That the common heritage of European values cannot be defined or limited by national boundaries was the essential point of the CSCE. North Americans and those Europeans who live on the fringes of the European continent are not so deeply touched by this vision. But for those who live hard by the now-vanished Iron Curtain, the idea of reuniting the Old Continent in peace and freedom has a powerful resonance. People in the streets of eastern Europe last year were moved by it. For divided Germany, the appeal is enormous and explains why the Bonn government has been in the vanguard of those who would give the Helsinki process a central and honored place in European diplomacy.

What does the CSCE—the Helsinki process—have to do with making Europe whole and free? If remembered at all by Americans, the Helsinki Final Act summons up images of surrendering eastern Europe to Soviet power in return for unenforceable promises on human rights—promises that Brezhnev ignored from the moment he affixed his signature to the document. "World War II is over—the Russians won," declared one pundit who even today considers the Final Act a great triumph for Soviet diplomacy. Gerald Ford signed the Final Act in 1975—and it probably hurt his chances for election to the presidency in 1976. Americans of East European descent thought Ford had condemned their ancestral lands to eternal servitude in a Soviet jailhouse. As it seemed to them, the smell of defeat and shabby expedience hung over the proceedings in Helsinki.

Those who still hold that view should look at the signatures of some of those who were present in Helsinki on August 1, 1975: Erich Honecker, Todor Zhivkov, Janos Kadar, Nicolae Ceausescu, Gustav Husak. Every one of them is now discredited, some have been imprisoned, one was executed, essentially for depriving their people of the freedom to live according to the principles of democracy and human rights enshrined in the Helsinki Final Act—for defying the ideal of a Europe whole and free. Is it too much to make the connection between the Helsinki process and the downfall of despots? Did the revolutions of 1989 happen despite the Helsinki Final Act? Ask the dissidents who were imprisoned for demanding that their governments fulfil the obligations of Helsinki. Ask the Helsinki Watch Committees throughout eastern Europe.

Ask the East Germans who were able to flee to the West because a new Hungarian government put more stock in its obligations under the CSCE than in the nation's previous agreements with the East German government.

A report in *The Washington Post* helps to explain how much is owed to the inspiration of the Final Act for what finally happened in 1989. On March 18, the *Post* noted, 1500 Czechoslovak Charter 77 activists were able to meet openly in Prague for the first time in the history of their movement. These people had been persecuted by their former government simply for asking, in a Charter they signed in January 1977, that it live up to the Helsinki accords. "Signing the Charter," as this news report recalled, "frequently spelled dismissal from employment, detention or imprisonment and denial of university education for one's children." Today, many members of Charter 77, including President Václav Havel, are among the leaders of democratic Czechoslovakia.

The first step toward a Europe whole and free was to deny the premise that there were two Europes. The Final Act was crammed full of affirmations about the rights of families to be reunified, of citizens to travel, of journalists to ply their trade, of people to have access to books and films. At the heart of the Final Act was the idea that Europe and North America are a single community consisting not merely of 35 states with their sovereign rights, but also of people with their own rights, needs, and aspirations. The promise of the Helsinki process was, and is, a Europe free of unnatural barriers and rich in the diversity which has always been its hallmark. And thus, breaking down walls was only a prelude to affirming a common heritage—freedom of thought, conscience, and religion and the right to self-determination free from outside interference.

Indeed, ideas have consequences. But to help guarantee consequences, the Final Act required follow-up meetings both to review implementation of its provisions and to expand the scope of cooperation. The first follow-up meeting, held at Belgrade, established the principle that the Helsinki Final Act was not a finished product, but rather the beginning of a process. Subsequent review meetings at Madrid and Vienna firmly established the principle of accountability, and numerous experts' meetings widened the possibilities for cooperative relations envisaged in the accords of 1975. The Final Act is not a treaty, and the process never has spawned an international bureaucracy, but the review meetings have become days—in fact, weeks and months—of reckoning from which no nation escapes. More important still are the citizen groups in many countries who, day-in, day-out, have dramatized violations and demanded compliance with the provisions of the Final Act.

If the process launched at Helsinki in 1975 has had such dire effects upon the Stalinist system—in the USSR, as well as in eastern Europe—why did Brezhnev sign the accords? Very likely because he saw the Final Act as American critics also saw it. He believed it would confirm the frontiers resulting from World War II and especially the division of Germany. In return for this, Brezhnev was willing to sign a document which was loaded with obligations which he probably thought communist governments would never have to fulfil and which, in fact, did not even acknowledge the legitimacy of territorial acquisitions imposed by force. He made several major miscalculations.

First, he overestimated the Soviet Union's ability to control the governments and peoples of eastern Europe. Second, he failed to anticipate the extent to which the human rights and humanitarian provisions of the Final Act would take on a life of their own. Third, he accepted a follow-on process, the agenda of which he could not bend exclusively to his own interests. Fourth, he legitimized a forum in which non-Soviet members of the Warsaw Pact could begin to exercise a modest degree of independence in their dealings with the West. Fifth, he failed to foresee the tenacity with which the North Americans and the West Europeans would pursue the matter of Soviet and East European compliance with the Final Act. His most fundamental error was to fail to understand the need for reform in the Soviet Union and to align his own government's policies with the principles of *Glasnost'* and democracy laid down in the Final Act.

Brezhnev, it is plain to see now, did not succeed in using the Helsinki Final Act to ratify the results of World War II, in the sense of guaranteeing that eastern Europe would be forever communist and under tight control from Moscow, or even in his aim of ensuring the perpetual division of Germany. What, then, explains Mikhail Gorbachev's interest in the Helsinki process? Gorbachev, like Brezhnev before him, is urging the West to join Moscow in advancing the CSCE process, but Gorbachev has a more spacious sense of what Soviet sacrifices in World War II bought for the Soviet people. In contrast to Brezhnev, who thought of CSCE in *status quo* terms, Gorbachev has a more dynamic view of the world. He sees a role for the CSCE in helping to create and give form to the new Europe. Does he hope to use the Helsinki process as an instrument to bring about the demise of NATO? Is he seeking ways to restore Soviet dominion over eastern Europe? Or is he looking to the CSCE to slow down the drive for German unification? Those pundits who are chronically suspicious of what they see as the misbegotten off-spring of craven European diplomacy and Nixonian cynicism already have suggested that such motives lie behind Gorbachev's interest in the CSCE.

The reasons behind Gorbachev's advocacy of a pan-European security system—an expanded, more institutionalized version of the system created by the Helsinki Final Act—are probably not grounded in altruism or naivete. Gorbachev no doubt is seeking a form of "droit de regard" over events in Europe. The Soviet Union's basic interests require Soviet leaders to have such a policy. Perhaps Gorbachev is counting on the ultimate dissolution of NATO, especially since the Warsaw Pact hardly exists any more. He probably seeks to expand Soviet influence at the expense of American, since Soviet influence is at a low ebb. But there are other explanations for Gorbachev's interest in CSCE. Moscow could become almost irrelevant to Europe as the European Community gains in political and economic strength and as the coin of Soviet military strength declines in value. Since military confrontation with the West and oppression in eastern Europe clearly do not serve Soviet security interests, Soviet leaders must find other ways to engage the West in order to influence developments of concern to Moscow. They may also see considerable advantage in an arrangement that would permit the Soviet Union and the United States to cooperate in limited ways within a common framework to promote stability in Europe.

Gorbachev has been emphatic in declaring that the United States and Canada should be a part of the European process. The corollary of this is that so should the Soviet Union. Soviet diplomacy gives the impression that Moscow rather wistfully hopes that the Warsaw Pact will survive in altered form to give the USSR a voice in East European affairs and that NATO therefore also could give the Americans influence in western Europe. But an acceptable alternative, so it seems, is to seek influence through the CSCE, rather than through the two alliances. If the CSCE is one method of projecting Soviet influence in Europe, does this mean that the process must be antithetical to western interests? Probably there would be greater danger for the West if Moscow were to conclude that there was no structural framework within which the Soviet Union could pursue its interests in Europe. To avoid that sense of injustice and offended pride which engenders conflict among nations it will be necessary to find some mechanism which allows each of them to have a proper share in the shaping of events and to strike a "balance of interests." Great nations cannot forever be relegated to the sidelines, whatever form the new Europe assumes.

The European members of the Atlantic alliance, and first among them, the Federal Republic of Germany, share Moscow's interest in the Helsinki process. They believe that this all-European, non-bloc negotiating forum already has made East-West cooperation possible in humanitarian, cultural, security, and other fields. They see the Helsinki process as one of the factors contributing to the tearing down of barriers between eastern and western Europe. The attraction of the idea of Europe whole and free is powerful. The European Community and NATO have contributed mightily to the realization of that dream but those institutions never can embrace the whole of Europe. And the CSCE was "made in Europe": the Final Act was very largely the product of West European diplomacy; West Europeans have been major players in all of the CSCE meetings held since then. Probably the Europeans also have concluded that Gorbachev's interest in the CSCE warrants a positive response from the West.

Where do the European members of the Atlantic alliance want to go with this process? There is talk of a European Confederation, an idea advanced by President Mitterrand of France (and by Henri IV in the seventeenth century). The CSCE could develop in this direction, although the President of France does not intend apparently, that the United States and Canada should be a part of this confederation. Other Europeans have different views about the roles of the superpowers and, at present, there really is no consensus in Europe about the future direction of the process. The politics of the CSCE is what interests Europeans, not any specific objective. Soviet leaders have been joined by many Europeans in supporting the CSCE as the basis for future all-European political developments. Whether logical or not, the CSCE very likely will be one of the chief instruments for putting in place the communications links among the several apartments that will constitute the "European home," and the obligations which will make "Europe whole and free."

But can the CSCE fulfil the large, if vague, expectations that have been placed upon it? In comparison with NATO or the European Community, the CSCE means little or nothing even to well-informed citizens of the United States and other nations somewhat removed from direct involvement in the events of the eastern part of the European continent. The CSCE has not acquired important public constituencies in most countries, always excepting its human rights aspects. Why, then, construct a new European system on a foundation which has so little public support? One answer is that there is no plausible alternative. Some formal structure in which North America and the Soviet Union can share with Europeans in the shaping of the European future probably will be necessary. In theory, new European institutions could be created. The European Community, through its associations agreements, and NATO, through its participation in a verification system to monitor troop cuts across the European continent, could help to construct pan-European institutions. Some linkage between NATO and the Warsaw Treaty Organization, or between more politically oriented successors to the two institutions is conceivable. None of these alternatives is likely to be so attractive that it will pull significant support away from the CSCE. The European Community is insufficiently universal in geographic and functional scope. A model based on NATO-Warsaw Pact cooperation does not square completely with realities in eastern Europe, where "blocs" are suspect. By itself, NATO can encourage the process of unifying Europe by creating conditions of reassurance supportive of German unity and by furnishing a sense of security to the maturing European Community. This NATO role would reinforce but not replace the CSCE.

A more positive answer to "why the CSCE?" is that while grass-roots name recognition may have escaped it until now,

CSCE exists and support for it is growing all over Europe. It is a familiar arrangement for most national decision makers. It is chartered to deal with every aspect of international and human life. The breadth and the flexibility are there to shape the future of Europe. It is a unifying process—inclusive rather than exclusive, and future-oriented, rather than focused on the premises of the cold war. And there is a need for all-European cooperation, perhaps especially after the East European revolutions of 1989. Aside from the "backsliding" from these democratic revolutions, a concern of the U.S. secretary of state, the opportunities for and the habit of engaging in active, sustained cooperation are important to nurture; this the CSCE uniquely can do on a European-Soviet-North American scale.

Some prominent Americans have ridiculed the "cumbersome" negotiating and decision-making procedures of the CSCE. The one thing that anyone who has ever heard of the CSCE knows is that Malta once blocked agreement against the wishes of all the other nations. But the image of diplomats mired in endless wrangles is wrong. Since 1975, many review meetings and specialized conferences have taken place. Consensus has been achieved in nearly every case. The Helsinki process has most of the same infuriating characteristics that any democratically organized deliberative body possesses. Like the American governmental system, it was not designed for efficiency, but it does work.

One view of the Europe of the future—especially in the United States—is that NATO and the CSCE represent different, and contradictory, ideas about the organization of Europe. Since NATO suits the interests of the United States, the CSCE is therefore in opposition to American interests. The rationale for this judgment is that American influence in NATO is strong, that the western democracies can cooperate effectively and efficiently within that structure, and that support for some form of all-European cooperative structure could only erode American influence in Europe. An intense and creative involvement in NATO by the United States is essential for the equilibrium of Europe. Support for NATO, however, is entirely compatible with an active American role in building a broader European-North American structure of international relations. Complementarity among NATO, the European Community, and the CSCE exists today and can exist in the future. There is no need for a triage. At the end of World War I, short-sighted policies led to catastrophe. A "Versailles" approach to the ending of the cold war could have similar results. Eastern Europe cannot be treated like a dory bobbing along in the wake of a western luxury liner if a "Europe whole and free" is to be born. And Gorbachev was being neither excessively chauvinistic nor merely magnanimous when he spoke to the Council of Europe in July 1989:

> The USSR and the United States are a natural part of the European international political structure. And their participation in its evolution is not only justified but also historically conditioned. Any other approach is unacceptable; and will not yield anything anyway.

There are serious questions, of course, as to whether the CSCE can play a major role in dealing with security problems in Europe or whether its contribution, while helpful, will be only marginal. These revolve around whether:

- It can be flexible enough to accommodate subregional arrangements within its framework. An inspection system for a 23-nation conventional force reduction agreement is one example; other requirements (crisis management and conciliation systems, e.g.) may emerge in eastern and southern Europe.
- It can be adapted to become an efficient and fast-moving operational institution. Dealing promptly with cross-border ethnic strife might be an example of what European security may mean in the future.
- It can provide scope for integrating movements within Europe which do not include the superpowers. The European Community is one obvious example; a defense force based on the Western European Union is another.
- It can become a cooperative security regime strong enough to accommodate and absorb realignments in power relations. A united Germany in NATO and a substantial withdrawal of U.S. and Soviet military forces from Central Europe are relevant examples.

These are the issues which will determine the future role of the CSCE in enhancing the security and stability of Europe and North America. Only time, good will, and a great deal of skillful diplomacy will resolve questions like these. At the moment, it is by no means clear that the CSCE could evolve sufficiently to adapt to the security problems of the new Europe.

Few would dispute that power—political, economic, and military power—is the key to the future ordering of European-North American relations. It is precisely this elemental force which seems to be missing from the contribution that the CSCE could make to peace and stability in Europe, according to most of the growing literature on the architecture of Europe. This verdict is not altogether wrong but it neglects the fact that countervailing power never has been a condition sufficient for maintaining peace and security and that it will become less dominant the next few decades as the postwar order collapses.

The end of the bipolar American-Soviet balance of power system has been announced periodically by geopolitically inclined scholars and politicians for two decades. Their hour finally has come—multipolarity has arrived. Now what's to be done with it? Only one thing is certain. In a multipolar world, maintaining an equilibrium among the principal power centers is a far more complex and subtle affair than in a bipolar system, placing far greater demands on statecraft and diplomacy.

Governments are groping—a more self-assured verb would not be accurate—for ways to regulate and channel emerging power realities. Alliances and institutional frameworks which were created during the cold war period are among the first instruments to which they have turned, even as they acknowledge that the character of these international arrangements will require radical change. One fundamental precept enjoys almost unanimous support in western Europe: the American presence in Europe should be maintained in tangible ways for the foreseeable future. The consensus on this point has balance of power considerations at its roots. The United States is still seen as a necessary weight in the balance of power equation despite the apparent shift of power between East and West and within western Europe. And the American presence should include military forces on the continent because the Soviet Union, a nuclear-armed continental power occupying the bulk of the Eurasian land mass, is not matched in sheer geopolitical terms by any combination of European nations.

This means that NATO should remain a vigorous institution on the European scene regardless of what has happened to the Warsaw Pact.

There are also sound practical reasons for this conclusion. One of the few indisputable facts about the current situation was bluntly stated by President Gorbachev. In his inaugural speech of March 15, 1990, President Gorbachev remarked that "The cold war has been done away with, but the military confrontation has not been overcome." It is a good guess that military confrontation in some form will continue even after the conclusion of the treaties on nuclear and conventional force reductions (START and Conference on Conventional Forces in Europe, or CFE). Another good guess is that political instability in the eastern part of the European continent will remain part of the scene for many years to come. President Bush was right to remark in his Camp David press conference on February 25, 1990, that: "The enemy is unpredictability. The enemy is instability." A shift in the balance of power in favor of the West does not signal the end of disorder and conflict, even in Europe.

A second point on which there is near unanimity is that the European Community must continue to provide an integrating framework for western Europe. It will be a very long time before the Community can be compared to a nation-state, either as a military power or as a quasi-unitary actor. But for all its administrative awkwardness and uneven institutional development the Community will use its economic and political power to exert influence on the world around it. While adding to the preponderance of political and economic power residing in the West, the Community also will contribute to the demise of the bipolar system and the consolidation of multipolarity, for it cannot be doubted that the Community will successfully exert influence in a westerly as well as an easterly direction.

Something is missing from this snapshot of the balance of power system which may emerge from the evolutionary development of NATO and the European Community. Nowhere in the picture does it show how Europe can truly become whole and free. It is a *status quo* approach to a highly fluid situation. It offers no vision of opportunities to construct a security system in which power is constrained not just by countervailing power but by the exercise of democratic control over national decisions. The Vienna conferences on conventional force reductions and confidence-building measures operate under the auspices of the CSCE, but security in Europe is not just a question of military limitations and reductions. The essence of European security lies in the process of creating an inclusive community of democratic nations. This is the special genius of the CSCE and this is the way in which the CSCE process can contribute to building a new European security system. As foreseen by the philosopher Immanuel Kant in 1795, a system in which democracy is the norm tends to promote peaceful relations among its members. In this sense, free elections are as much a security measure as ceilings on tanks.

The system that is beginning to emerge from the Helsinki process may serve to restrain power even before the triumph of democracy in every corner of Europe. At the end of the Napoleonic wars a system of cooperative security was constructed based on a coalition of the great powers. Statesmen of that day firmly believed in balance of power diplomacy. But many of them also believed that their common interests in maintaining an equilibrium in Europe required strict limits on the use of force for purely national ends. These statesmen, therefore, sought to moderate and resolve the inevitable threats to that equilibrium through the device of frequent multilateral conferences supplemented, of course, by behind-the-scenes negotiations in smaller groups. The Concert of Europe, created in 1815, lasted only until 1822 in its original incarnation but the notion of a collective responsibility for European security continued to exert influence, even across ideological fault lines, through much of the nineteenth century. Only rarely throughout the hundreds of years of the nation-state system in Europe have conditions favored development of a concert system. The 1990s seemingly will mark the end of a long period of bitter, ideological hostility and of the bipolar system which grew up in that period. The next several years may see a gradual reemergence of the concert system, whether consciously designed or not, mainly because war does not seem to be a very likely or useful policy alternative. Interdependence has proceeded very far in western Europe and between North America and western Europe. The western nations have learned that interdependence does not bring an end to disputes but that it does create the need for mechanisms constantly at work to head off or resolve conflicts, as well as to foster the undeniable benefits of interdependence. A concert system might develop in parallel with the spread of interdependence in all its aspects throughout Europe simply because it will become more, rather than less necessary, as shared values and interests begin to take hold across the Old Continent. Experimenting with such a system need not and should not weaken the ties among the old democracies. Erosion of "psychological dividing lines," a problem cited by Henry Kissinger (*Washington Post*, April 15, 1990), is a low-order risk in the short term if only because few governments will be ready to scrap something they know for something with which they are unfamiliar until time has given evidence that the essentials for a concert system are in place. In the long term, shouldn't the object of policy of the democratic nations be precisely that of eroding psychological dividing lines by encouraging the growth of democratic institutions everywhere in Europe?

The CSCE comes close to matching the institutional characteristics of a concert system. A concert system is based on the assumptions of:

- Shared interests, including a desire to preserve the system;
- Openness within the system;
- Expectations of cooperative behavior by participating states and a "feed-back" mechanism to encourage needed corrections;
- Available means of validating intentions;
- A mechanism for restoring equilibrium in response to disturbances in the system.

In rudimentary, unfulfilled form most of these elements can be discerned in the CSCE process which, after all, is still evolving. Openness and methods of validating perceptions already exist in the current European environment and in the CSCE process, but need strengthening. The CSCE's main accomplishment has been to set norms for expected behavior and build pressures for compliance. The Helsinki process, however, has not had to face real crises which could test how effectively the CSCE could restore equilibrium to a system in disarray. Up to the present time, the CSCE's essential role has been to promote a common value system throughout Europe. Only time will tell how broad and deep the commitment to European cooperation really is and whether the CSCE could become the framework for a concert system. Out of the wreck-age of the hegemonic system in eastern Europe—and in the Soviet Union, too—a more democratic system ultimately will emerge. But unfinished business in Central and eastern Europe, and in the Soviet Union, means that domestic and international political arrangements necessary to justify confidence in shared values and interests have not yet appeared. Europe is not yet ready for a concert system—and certainly not for one which would replace existing institutions—but the CSCE offers a good basis for testing the possibilities, and for developing the institutional infrastructure. The CSCE should be seen and used in this light.

There will be no shortage of opportunities to test the capacity of the CSCE to deal with problems of the power equilibrium in Europe. One of the safer assumptions in mid-1990 is that Germany will unite during 1991, that she will become even more dominant within the European Community than she is already, and that the European Community will gain political and economic ascendancy in eastern Europe. The balance of power in Europe, in the measures of merit that count the most these days, is shifting in ways that must have important consequences. The Atlantic alliance and the European Community together serve to channel power within a western framework. United Germany must remain solidly within this framework, in the view of all western governments. This is not the publicly expressed opinion of the Soviet government, however, and Germany is the object of much diplomatic maneuvering. This is hardly surprising since Germany is the net gainer in European power terms. This is well understood by the Germans, who know the huge stakes involved.

As the drive for German unification has gathered momentum it is evident that the place of united Germany in Europe has assumed greater weight in Moscow's thinking about the Helsinki process. Soviet spokesmen use the word "synchronized" to describe the relation between German unification and the further development of the CSCE. "A European Germany, not a German Europe," a phrase of Thomas Mann's, quoted approvingly by Shevardnadze and Genscher, captures the essence of the problem. It is in this context that much of Moscow's recent comment about the CSCE has been offered. Probably Gorbachev and Shevardnadze entertain some hopes that the CSCE could become a grand entente, or European concert within which their worries about a united Germany could be shared and assuaged. And so it could become. But united Germany should be a key actor in such a system, and not as a neutral but as a leading member of a democratic coalition.

Whether or not a true concert ever emerges from it, the CSCE is well positioned to deal with security issues related to a united Germany. It can do so by ensuring that binding obligations concerning military matters are broadly based. To ask the Germans alone to take on obligations stemming from an assumption that democratic Germany is a threat to the peace would be to sow the seeds of future trouble. Restraints on military forces aimed at Germany alone are not justified and would have harmful long-run politico-psychological effects.

Reductions and limitations on conventional military forces should apply generally, not just to Germany. The same is true of nuclear weapons. Obligations that the Federal Republic of Germany already has undertaken with regard to nuclear weapons were balanced by NATO arrangements which provided for the nuclear defense of German territory and, in the context of the Nuclear Non-proliferation Treaty, by an obligation of the signatory nuclear powers to seek nuclear disarmament. All of these obligations must be maintained by all the parties to them; a united Germany should assume the same obligation. Although their governments may continue to object, the new situation—post-German unification and post-START treaty—will require Britain and France to think again about entering negotiations to reduce their nuclear forces. These considerations point to the future security agenda of the CSCE.

In the case of conventional force levels and verification of those levels, the 23 nations in the CFE already are negotiating the necessary treaty obligations affecting those nations. The CSCE also could provide an organizational home for the verification system and take note of the obligations assumed by 23 of the participants to accept:

- Ceilings on levels of military forces, including major items of equipment;
- Understandings related to the operations of these forces;
- The means of assuring that compliance with these obligations can be verified.

All 35 of the CSCE participants negotiating in the Vienna Conference on Confidence- and Security-Building Measures could assume obligations to accept:

- Transparency of military operations and some constraints on those operations;
- An exchange of information concerning their defense budgets.

Depending on their nuclear status, all the CSCE participants also could pledge:

- Not to acquire nuclear weapons; or
- To accelerate progress toward limitations on and reductions in stocks of nuclear weapons.

Treaty commitments in some cases would have to supplement the political commitments which have been the standard and only means of recording agreements in CSCE up to now, but this is not to say that all 35 participants in the CSCE would have to be involved in all the negotiations and obligations or be bound by all of them. It is not desirable to shift the whole CSCE process from the realm of politically binding accords to that of a legally binding treaty. Cooperation has proceeded very well in many fields without benefit of treaty obligations. An exception, however, might be all or some of the ten principles of the Helsinki Final Act "guiding relations between participating states," which could provide the basis for a treaty commitment among the 35. In conjunction with certain other treaty obligations that may be negotiated in the "two-plus-four" talks, such a treaty could have beneficial effects on the currently uneasy climate in Europe, particularly if it confirmed the precise frontiers of united Germany.

These and certain other undertakings, perhaps also in treaty form, could begin to build an institutional infrastructure for what might eventually become a concert system including *all* 35 nations of the CSCE together with their subregional alliances. These other commitments could be aimed at strengthening the CSCE's procedures for restoring equilibrium, encouraging openness, and validating intentions. For example, the CSCE participants could agree to establish:

- Readily available means of conducting formal consultations, instituting conciliation procedures, and making enquiries regarding compliance with political obligations. An executive council could meet at the level of heads of government or at ministerial level.

- Means for conducting dialogue and discussion among elected representatives of the people of the 35 CSCE participating states. This might be a legislative council, modeled after the North Atlantic Assembly, a consultative forum of legislators of the Atlantic alliance.

Bureaucratizing the CSCE process through large secretariats is the last thing CSCE needs; setting up an executive council structure should avoid that. Ministers from CSCE participants would meet, perhaps frequently, during each year on the basis of an agenda worked out among capitals. Just as the European Community found it necessary to establish a "groupe des correspondants"—liaison officers, in effect, in each capital—so might the CSCE arrange a steering committee whose members would be resident in capitals. Through such a device the harmonizing, conciliating, and consulting functions of the CSCE could be strengthened without establishing huge bureaucracies.

Participants in meetings of an executive council need not be limited to heads of governments or ministers of foreign affairs, nor should it be necessary always to include every one of the 35 participants, if some form of accountability existed. Ministers responsible for the environment, transportation, culture, and all the other subjects covered by CSCE also could meet from time to time. The purpose of such meetings could include efforts to work out common policies and programs of action. This approach, which emphasizes cooperation and integration, is an entirely plausible use of the CSCE and is consistent with the traditions of the Helsinki process. It could pave the way for a true concert system in Europe.

Can the CSCE really help lay to rest the bitter legacies of the past and create conditions for a Europe—and a Germany—whole and free? Willy Brandt referred recently to the "Devil's Circle" that has entrapped Europe in this century. The CSCE, used in full recognition of its limits, but also of its possibilities, could break that Devil's Circle. And it would be best if a beginning were made this year. All of the obligations and international arrangements just mentioned can take effect within the framework afforded by CSCE. A CSCE summit meeting later this year might be able to agree on some of them and should provide a mandate to their negotiators to start working on those not yet ready for agreement. The results of their work could be taken up and put into operation at the next regularly scheduled review meeting of the CSCE in Helsinki in 1992, or even earlier if negotiations prosper.

II. European Security and Alliance Politics

Chapter 7

What Kind of European Architecture?

Michael Stürmer

When the Berlin Wall fell on November 9, 1989, the framework of the postwar security system fell as well, including the basic assumptions of conventional arms control in Europe. Three factors had come together. First, Gorbachev's "Second Russian Revolution" with all its ambiguities and uncertainties; second, the East European revolutions; third, and most important, the German revolution of last summer and fall, upsetting the security landscape in Europe.

The cold war is over, or nearly so, and the West has prevailed. A system of high configuration and high calculability is giving way to a situation of—for the time being—low confrontation coupled with low calculability. How does the new European configuration, with Germany uniting and the Soviets retreating, affect the rationale of the Atlantic alliance and the role of the United States in Europe, and what kind of long-term European security system should we aim for? The answer has three parts:

- The threat recedes, but this is not the end of history;
- The silent agenda of the North Atlantic Treaty Organization (NATO) is changing but will not disappear;
- Security will continue to be needed, and there is nothing to replace the Atlantic alliance.

A Receding Threat

In the past, Soviet forces in eastern Europe, altogether about 600,000 men, served four politico-military functions:

- To support communist oligarchies that tended to administer their respective countries more or less in a satellite sense, and to save them in time of crisis. This was called the Brezhnev Doctrine, but it had been invented by Stalin: the bilateral mutual assistance agreements, administered by the Warsaw Pact, served as an instrument of control and intervention.
- To threaten western Europe and to hold the West Europeans hostage against the United States. The Soviets always tried to keep two options open: Blitzkrieg after short warning time and full-scale attack preceded by long warning time. But the U.S. presence and nuclear deterrence denied both of them.
- To keep the inner empire together through control of the outer empire; and
- To guard the glacis of the motherland and to secure the delivery of goods and services to the Soviet Union while forced labor from occupied territories went out of fashion after Stalin.

Today, most of the Red Army troops are still in place, but they have lost most of their political role and military significance. The withdrawal of 50,000 men and 5,000 tanks announced by Gorbachev on December 7, 1988, in the United Nations seems to be on the way. It takes away the cutting edge of the threat and enhances the West's warning time. Moreover, Soviet troops have lost the secure—if not friendly—environment they once enjoyed. Their supply lines are overstretched. While the forthcoming Conventional Forces in Europe (CFE) agreement will have to take away not only the excess of 195,000 Russians agreed in Ottawa, it will also put the remainder in a precarious position: they will be too little to see them in a serious military role, too much to ignore their political veto role, their nuisance value in the course of German unification, and the burden they put on crisis stability. It must surely be the West's aim, in the next round of CFE, to reduce their presence to zero without delay, leaving behind only an agreed number of verification experts. Meanwhile it should not be forgotten that in the European theater the cold war was, above all, the conflict over the German succession. Now this succession is open, once again, and with it the familiar question of Europe hegemony. If the answer is not a

European and Atlantic one, it can only be Russian or German. The fate of Germany is going to be the crucial East-West issue over the next five years, until the Russians have moved away from the Elbe and the Oder.

In this crisis, however, the Russians have more than one script to follow:

- The first script would be a benign and stability oriented one, starting from a major quid pro quo with the West in its entirety and full Soviet acceptance of Germany's continuing membership in NATO and the European Community with appropriate western self-restraint in eastern Germany much as the Norwegians practice in their northernmost province.
- The second script would be less benign and more irrational: a return to the late nineteenth century Franco-Russian alliance coupled with the continuation of as much as possible of four power control resulting, in its turn, in a German revolt, the demise of NATO, and the evisceration of the European Community.
- A third script would have equal, but opposite historical antecedents. It would repeat, as Gorbachev does at present, Stalin's 1952 unity-for-neutrality offer, wreck Germany's western integration, and aim for a long-term partnership between Russia and Germany similar to that growing out of the 1922 Treaty of Rapallo.

At present, only the first, benign scenario seems to be in the enlightened self-interest of the Soviets. But it needs a firm hand in Washington and imaginative leadership in other western capitals to prevail. Otherwise, Germany will be put into the position of the proverbial loose cannon on deck, and the result will be condominium over Germany, or a new confrontation between East and West.

Meanwhile, it should not be overlooked that among the implicit functions of Russian forces in eastern Europe was their peacekeeping role in countries traditionally haunted by economic backwardness, ethnic strife, and political weakness. Now that the iron lid has been thrown off, some of the old demons of the 1920s will be seen again, causing both new insecurity and the need for peacekeeping of a more enlightened kind.

NATO's Silent Agenda

NATO came into being for the purpose of double containment: of the German past and the Soviet present. In the course of time, this turned into a double balance. The United States, by providing reassurance and deterrence, kept the strategic East-West balance much as the political West-West balance. Thus, far beyond its explicit and immediate military appearance and posture, NATO always had an invisible agenda both in terms of politics and psychology.

Lord Ismay, NATO's first Secretary General, hinted at this agenda when saying that NATO was invented to keep the Russians out, the Americans in, and the Germans down. Whatever the wider implications of the third point, the following functions stand out as important parts of NATO's seldom spoken agenda:

- To prevent U.S. withdrawals of the 1920 type and make the United States, as a kind of "fleet in being," the guaranteeing force for western Europe's industrial democracies;
- To couple European security from the Elbe to the Irish Sea to the strategic nuclear potential of the United States;
- To offer to France and Germany the chance of reconciliation, much as to the other European nations haunted by the past;
- To turn the German question from a divisive burden into the engine of West European integration;
- To protect the European neutral and nonaligned states from being overshadowed by the Soviet Union and finding their neutrality made hollow;
- To take on board the two Iberian former dictatorships and help these new democracies safeguard against the return of history;
- To protect the decline of the former imperial powers, France and Britain, without violence and upheaval;
- To limit nuclear proliferation by extending nuclear protection—this is a function more important than ever before in the 1990s; and
- To promote and organize arms control and stabilize it without loss of security.

All these items are still on the agenda, some have definitely gained in importance. The European Community (EC) finds in

NATO its inconspicuous security framework. And without the North Americans firmly tied to Europe, the Conference on Security and Cooperation in Europe (CSCE) chessboard would be little more than a hunting preserve for the Soviets.

Security Needs Continue

The question of security relates directly to the rationale for NATO. Can NATO be replaced, in part or as a whole? Three preliminary answers tend to be passed around: the CSCE, the European Community, or the Western European Union.

In the past, CSCE has been a diplomatic congress, coming together from time to time to try to balance eastern, western, neutral, and nonaligned concerns. The Helsinki Final Act of 1975 with its three baskets—acceptance of the political status quo, expansion of commerce, and respect for human rights— was helpful to promote change. But it was not a legal, binding document. Today, there are some who think that the CSCE could and should be turned into a system of collective security in Europe. But collective security can only work where a community of values and interests exists as well as a balance of forces. With an oversized empire such as the Soviet Union involved, this is difficult to imagine. Moreover, collective security promises that everybody is allied with everybody else, and in reality that means that nobody is allied with anybody. An important point to remember is that the North Americans are in Europe via NATO, and only via NATO, and it would be difficult to inspire in Congress and American public opinion the same deep-rooted loyalties for CSCE that NATO has secured and will—if NATO reform is managed and properly advertised—continue to encourage.

In the future, CSCE can and must deepen, and with Japan showing interest, it should widen. But it should not be overburdened by collective security: in this case it would be another League of Nations and nothing but a contemporary version of the sad old tale of how the vision of collective security turns into the reality of collective insecurity, power vacuum, and hegemony. In the future, starting at the 1990 summit, CSCE could and should develop an institutional framework, such as Germany's Foreign Minister Hans-Dietrich Genscher has hinted at various instances in the recent past, and some of these institutions should be housed in the city of Berlin:

- Coordination of East-West economic cooperation, including a link to the European Bank for Reconstruction and Development;
- A watchdog function for human rights, underlining the human rights catalogue of the Council of Europe;
- A center for overseeing the development of respect for the state of law in European states;
- A European environment agency;
- An expansion of the Eurêka high technology project for the whole of Europe;
- The cooperation of the European Space Agency (ESA) with the respective institutions in the East;
- A center for the development of a European telecommunications structure;
- A center for developing a European infrastructure for transportation systems; and
- Most important a European center of conflict management and of arms control verification.

If collective security is not a possibility through the CSCE, could and should the European Community play a defense role? The European Community agenda is already heavily overburdened by the 1992 process, by the creation of the European Monetary Union (EMU), by the assistance needed in eastern Europe, and by German reunification. The European Community is the West's single most important instrument to influence peaceful change in eastern Europe. But giving it a defense role would provoke deep-seated resentment among the European nuclear powers, give the wrong signal to the United States, and weaken NATO's coherence. A defense role for the European Community will surely overburden it and make it far less efficient at a time when it is needed more than ever before in other roles.

What about the Western European Union? It has too long been waiting for the prince's kiss to encourage much hope that this time the miracle will happen. The Western European Union can in fact function as a component of NATO, but not the outside organization of the European Community, or a politico-military directorate. The dramatic new divergences between Britain's and France's nuclear status and Germany's nonnuclear role alone are sufficient to explain why. West European political integration will probably receive a boost from the 1989 revolutions. But, at the same time, given Germany's focal role, French policymakers will remember de Gaulle's classic statement that: "Nuclear weapons cannot be shared."

So we are left with three basic assumptions: First, the Soviet threat has indeed diminished but it has given way to revolutionary instability, with no small number of old demons in eastern Europe coming out of their graves and a detachment of apocalyptic horsemen, called the new global challenges, galloping across the stage.

Second, Europe's security architecture is still based on the double balance of West-West and East-West, both parts of which the United States has kept in the past, but its future management needs more active participants, more political finesse, and less military hardware.

And, third, NATO's invisible agenda has been extended to include a measure of long-term reassurance for the Soviets, coupled with the careful management of Soviet decline and political support for the East Europeans coming out of the cold.

For the United States, Europe after the Wall has gained in political, strategic, and economic importance, but also in complexity. It is now, once again, the place where the balance of the world is being decided and where the international order of the twenty-first century is being shaped. In this, the United States not only plays a decisive role. It also has a vital interest at stake. NATO is still, and will be even more so in the future, the most effective and most subtle framework within which those interests can be brought to bear. But NATO without a firm U.S. presence in Europe would be hollow both in military and political terms.

For the foreseeable future, the integration of united Germany and the decline of Soviet power will be the most important issues of European architecture, and they can only be solved in conjunction with both arms control and NATO reform. As far as arms control is concerned, a quid pro quo seems to be reasonable, offering the Russians agreements on strategic nuclear, conventional, and chemical weapons and an "open skies" verification agreement in addition to Coordinating Committee for Multilateral Export Controls concessions and some sizable help in their reconstruction. In return, the

West would insist on united Germany's continued membership in NATO, with suitable self-restraints in the eastern provinces and a European verification regime housed in Berlin.

As far as NATO is concerned, the invisible agenda will become even more important. While troop numbers will go down, NATO must make sure that the scramble for the peace dividend does not become counterproductive and, indeed, destructive. Now is the time to wind up the kind of arms control shaped by cold war and confrontation and to design the role of arms and arms control for the security architecture of the next century. At reduced numbers, NATO's reinforcement capability in Europe is even more necessary than in the past. It is surely more important than the numbers game, and it must determine the bottom line of troop reductions. In the nuclear dimension NATO will have to give up land-based short-range nuclear forces (SNF) much as it has done with intermediate-range nuclear forces (INF). Even more important, the next phase of the strategic arms reduction talks (START) will have to include the concept of existential deterrence that would be based upon a residual force of about 2,000 warheads on each side and would ensure that the long nuclear peace of the postwar decades is rationalized and preserved well into the next century.

Can anyone imagine that in this crisis of the world balance it would serve U.S. interests to withdraw into strategic ambiguity and insularity? The logic of the 1989 revolutions points in a different direction. Europe in general, Central Europe in particular, has acquired once again a focal role. The EC framework is becoming ever more important, but defense and security are beyond its limits. In order to prevent the CSCE from becoming another League of Nations, it must not be charged with a security role that it cannot play.

The United States must respond to the revolutionary changes in Europe not by taking long-term leave but by offering security and reassurance in both West-West and East-West terms. In this, NATO needs the United States as finder and lender of last resort. But the United States also needs NATO as the instrument to keep the double balance in Europe—and far beyond.

Chapter 8

Stability and Security in Europe: A French Point of View

Georges Vaugier

Speaking in present circumstances about European security, one has to be conscious that the most detailed plans risk being overtaken by events at the very moment that they are introduced. In this context, I want to make a few remarks reflecting a French point of view on the present situation and to present some ideas and concepts about security and stability on the continent already put forward by French authorities. Those ideas and concepts are not always well-known in this country, and are sometimes misunderstood.

Today it is widely recognized that the sweeping changes in the Soviet Union and eastern Europe are bringing the postwar system to a close and are clearing the way for the construction of a new system. Until recently Europe was divided between two blocks. The neutral countries played a weak role in European diplomacy. Within a few months the main elements of this system vanished. As an external result of Soviet *perestroika* and complementary to the internal changes in Moscow, the old communist leaders of eastern Europe, all of them, fell from power. Before too many months pass Soviet troops will withdraw from this area. Discussions are already under way on this subject with Prague and Budapest. The Warsaw Pact itself will also disappear, or at the very least lose all its military and political meaning. At the same time, on many levels, Germany is progressing at a quick pace toward its unification.

Today the geopolitical landscape in which we live has been almost totally transformed. The European-Atlantic world is now divided into four groups:

- The first includes the members of the European Community (EC) and the European members of the Atlantic alliance;
- The second group is composed of the neutral and non-aligned countries that are interested in playing an active role, in developing cooperation on a European scale;
- The third group comprises the former satellites of the Soviet Union, that are in the process of liberation and democratization; and
- The fourth group, the Soviet Union itself.

In these new conditions, the task is to determine what must be kept and what must be created to offer the best possible basis for stable long-term security.

The European Community as the Foundation

In the midst of all the uncertainty surrounding the future of the continent, almost everyone will agree that the European Community represents the most solid structure on which to build. That is why the French authorities are putting a particular emphasis on both the acceleration and the deepening of European integration among the twelve EC member states. They insist on the completion on schedule, that means by the beginning of 1993, of:

- The single market;
- The economic and monetary union; and
- The political union (which becomes necessary at this stage).

President François Mitterrand and Chancelor Helmut Kohl have recently made concrete proposals for achieving the political union. They specify four main objectives:

- To strengthen the democratic legitimacy of the union;
- To make the European institutions more efficient;
- To consolidate unity and cohesion in the economic, monetary, and political fields; and
- To define and conduct a common foreign and security policy.

In making the many changes necessary to achieve this unprecedented degree of integration, the European Community must concentrate on its own development. The magnitude of this task makes it impossible to accept any new members for the foreseeable future. The eastern part of Germany has been de facto a member of the Community through its free trade with West Germany, and its inclusion into the Federal Republic will not be an exception to the rule of no expansion before integration.

In the search for a more stable framework for the emerging democratic regimes in East Central Europe, President Mitterrand proposed in his New Year's address to the French people a new concept of a "European Confederation." It could be the expression of the great Europe of tomorrow, with multiparty democracy and the rule of law that protects basic human and political rights. Embracing all European countries of democratic government, this confederation could constitute a desirable goal for the future that would channel the aspirations of the former Soviet satellites and provide an institution to help them balance the strength of a unified Germany.

There is a place in this greater Europe for the Soviet Union. When the Warsaw Pact ceases to exist, when Soviet troops leave Germany and eastern Europe, the Soviet Union will remain a European state, with a legitimate interest in all major developments that affect the evolution of the European continent. When designing a confederation based on democratic principles—we find it entirely appropriate for the Soviet Union to take its place as a member when it has set up and confirmed free institutions itself.

At this point I should add that for discussion about the future of Europe the Conference on Security and Cooperation in Europe (CSCE) offers a well-adapted and useful forum. Indeed, in the framework of the Helsinki process important results have been achieved, concerning human rights and security. Security is a permanent matter for the thirty-five countries participating in the CSCE. Ties are being forged, and the Helsinki process must go on. New progress is possible, and various proposals are already circulating. On the French side, Foreign Minister Roland Dumas recently proposed that the CSCE should develop:

- A network of communications to permit the exchange of information on military maneuvers;

- Annual sessions for evaluating confidence-building and disarmament measures; and above all,
- A system to deal with crisis situations.

More generally, France has offered to host in Paris later this year a summit conference at which the thirty-five heads of state and government will be shaping new steps to expand European security and cooperation.

A Distinction between Security and Defense

While committed to the CSCE, the French government is convinced that CSCE can serve neither as the political model for a new Europe nor as a substitute for the Atlantic alliance. French analysis draws a basic distinction between security (which concentrates on arms control, confidence building, verification, and crisis prevention) and defense (which focuses on armaments, force structure, deployments, strategy, and alliances). Within this dichotomy, France relies primarily on the CSCE and, in coming years, on the European Community for its security and on its own national forces and on the Atlantic alliance for its defense.

Based on this analysis, France considers that the Atlantic alliance is vital for defense and remains an indispensable element of a stable Europe. On April 19, 1990, in Key Largo, Florida, President Mitterrand was very clear on this point: "The first thing for the Alliance is to maintain its cohesion, and in this respect it's necessary to reassert the need for the presence of United States forces in Europe."

The alliance as a community of values, as an organic framework for the cooperation between France and other European countries with the United States should be preserved. If the western alliance continues and the Warsaw Pact disintegrates, there will be an asymmetry between the security arrangements for East and West. But this is no reason to abandon a western system that works and for which there is a continued need. It should be recalled that the Atlantic alliance was established not as a counterpart to the Warsaw Pact which did not yet exist. Indeed the Soviet threat was the original cause of the forming of the alliance. Soviet intentions are peaceful now and it looks as if Soviet troops will return to home territory. Nevertheless, many factors are still troubling, among others a general uncertainty about the future, and the geographic asymmetry that provides much easier access to western Europe for the Soviet Union than for the United States. Tomorrow the Soviet Union will still appear as a military power, a nuclear power, and a continental power. No nation in Europe can match its strength, so there is a continuing rationale for the Atlantic alliance.

While the Soviet Union remains a potential threat, the overall range of threats facing the West is changing. It is appropriate for the alliance to initiate a new evaluation of its structure and strategy. But once more it is essential to avoid any confusion between defense and security. Security issues have their right place in the Helsinki framework. Defense matters have to be discussed inside the alliance.

France is prepared to take an active part in both groups this year, at the summit meeting of the thirty-five in Paris, as well as at the alliance summit to convene in July as President Mitterrand and President Bush agreed in Key Largo. One of the main topics will be to adapt the alliance to the new requirements and to prepare the Europeans for the idea of playing an increased role in providing for their own defense.

European Community, European confederation, Atlantic alliance, CSCE—each structure has its own purposes and value. The creation of a European confederation and new progress of the CSCE would facilitate the evolution in the eastern part of the continent where the transformation of Europe has moved most dramatically.

Chapter 9

European Security: The Case for Progressive Evolution

Air Vice Marshal R. A. Mason

The ferment of analysis and forecast which has accompanied events in Europe and the Soviet Union during the last nine months is a measure of concern felt on both sides of the Atlantic at their unpredictability, speed, and potential for destabilization. In focusing on "European security" I am well aware that you cannot achieve security by military power alone, but military power alone can seriously threaten it.

In making speculative remarks about future arrangements for security in Europe, I am pedantically uneasy about a search for new "systems" whose main components are at present difficult to define and close interrelationships infinitely more so. There are, in addition, two unhelpful future polarities. One fails to provide any overarching European security system at all. Existing security organizations become moribund and ineffectual; no alternative or additional structures are created, and security or the lack of it devolves on ad hoc bilateral or multilateral agreements which will ultimately rest on comparative national strength and not on any broader concepts of cooperation. In that way lies a return to 1939.

The second polarity is the hasty creation of a European security system intended to identify and resolve every conceivable source of instability in Europe in the foreseeable future. Such a structure would risk being ineffectual and inflexible and would introduce into Europe many of the weaknesses and inertia of an organization such as the United Nations without any of its virtues. Between those two extremes, however, there is a great deal of scope and opportunity.

The Future Security Environment

May I first explain my assumptions about the likely security environment in Europe and then suggest possible ingredients for a future security framework.

Hitherto it has been sufficient to note the year, and perhaps the month, on a conference paper in order to remind the reader of the circumstances and expectations then prevailing. Now we need a precise date—at least. Indeed, events have moved so quickly that in our determination to follow, analyze, and predict it is very easy to forget that despite all that has changed, all that is unpredictable, certain facts remain, and some predictions can be confidently classed as certainties. My assumptions begin with those, then shade through the probable to the problematical.

The first certainty is that the Soviet Union, whatever its future composition, will retain because of its proximity a keen and legitimate interest in security in Europe. That interest has traditional roots. One lies in the Soviet Union's lack of natural defensive frontiers with eastern Europe, and a concern that the region has always been a natural conduit for military adventures against Russia. I do not share the view that Soviet strategy after World War II was based on defensive considerations, but rather that the establishment of hegemony in the occupied countries was a coincidence of ideological and political expansionism which had at the same time the advantage of establishing a deep military defensive zone. The current Soviet regime appears to be coming to accept the fact that the North Atlantic Treaty Organization (NATO) does not present an offensive threat and that the political, economic, and military costs of sustaining such hegemony have become unsupportable. The underlying circumstances will however remain.

The other traditional root of Soviet concern lies in the potential for instability within eastern Europe itself which could, as in the years before 1939, be perceived as potentially damaging to Russian interests with or without the involvement of other powers. Any future system which does not accept the legitimacy of such interests, and does not make cooperative provision for their resolution, would risk the longer term possibilities of Russian revanchism.

The second certainty is that the Soviet Union will remain in one form or another the strongest military power in Europe. It will retain the largest army, the largest and best equipped air force, the largest navy, and the largest nuclear arsenal. Regardless of the outcome of the negotiations on Conventional Forces in Europe (CFE), and any unilateral withdrawal of forces from eastern Europe, the whole of Europe will remain within range of Soviet aircraft. Even with a reduction of resource allocation, *perestroika* will encourage the Soviet Air Forces to become better trained, more efficiently led, and in a position to operate modern equipment more effectively. In addition, CFE will leave Soviet force projection capabilities unimpaired.

The third certainty is that for the foreseeable future the only international instrument available to the Soviet Union will be military force. The nation is ideologically bankrupt, economically impotent, and increasingly dependent diplomatically on the goodwill of the West.

The fourth certainty is that the Warsaw Pact has already ceased to exist as a coordinated military organization capable of waging aggressive coalition warfare of a kind stipulated by Soviet doctrine for the last generation. Nor in the foreseeable future will it recover the ability to mount multinational operations. Unlike NATO, it does not possess in its present form the political infrastructure or consensus necessary for it to contribute toward a different kind of European security framework.

The fifth certainty is that German unification will take place. Whatever decision is made about the future military position of Germany (all within NATO, all neutral, or some half-and-half arrangement whereby NATO forces are not stationed in what is now the German Democratic Republic), it is impossible to imagine a Central European battleground on which German forces would oppose each other.

The sixth certainty is that a degree of economic and political cooperation has now been reached in western Europe to render any resolution of political differences there by military force unthinkable. Those who look back with concern to the Europe of 1914 as eastern Europe unravels in 1990 tend to overlook this considerable, and in European history unique, source of stability on the continent.

My seventh and final certainty is that beyond Europe the use of military force will not be renounced.

A further assumption is a prediction, which if implemented over a period of three years or so, will regardless of any other military developments in eastern Europe, fundamentally change the correlation of ground forces between East and West. The two major ingredients will be reduction to numerical parity within the theater in all major land-based conventional weapons systems, and the large impact of the associated verification regimes. Parity of forces does not in itself guarantee military stability. History is replete with examples of armed forces which by surprise, deception, superior tactics, training, etc., successfully initiated operations against numerically equal or superior opposition. After CFE it would be theoretically possible for residual Soviet forces in Central Europe to launch an attack, but without extensive reinforcement their objectives, whether territorial, punitive, or pre-emptive, would be limited in time and space. Moreover, for reasons already adduced, it is difficult to envisage Soviet forces having (non-Soviet Warsaw Pact) support in such action unless events had taken an unwelcome direction in a unified Germany.

It is, however, the interaction of parity and verification which provides the better guarantee of increased stability. The extent of verification required by the agreements will make clandestine reinforcement over anything but the shortest distances very difficult to achieve in Central Europe and virtually impossible from the western Soviet Union across eastern Europe. The alternative of overt preparation for a larger scale military excursion would presuppose political circumstances which are difficult to envisage in the foreseeable future.

In sum, the combined military implications for the West of an implemented CFE agreement will be a greatly reduced conventional, ground-based military threat and a lengthy warning time of any reconstitution of such a threat.

Flowing from those confident assumptions are others more problematical and uncertain, which make proposals for a new security system more tentative. The first obviously concerns the immediate and longer term position of a unified Germany which has the economic potential to become a regional super-power. In the short term the question is how to absorb the new Germany within the existing security structures. The longer term answer may or may not be the same one. In the short term, the proposal to retain NATO forces in West Germany, while greatly reduced Soviet troops remain across what is now the inner German border, seems the least difficult to apply, but that view is not necessarily shared in either Bonn or Berlin. It would be accompanied by the maintenance for a transitional period of separate German armed forces but would allow a two-stage approach to the overall problem: first devising an internal organization to bring both sets of armed forces together, and then, within a broader framework reaching an agreement on the overall size of the unified forces. One possibility would be the early reduction of conscription and the creation of much smaller, professional armed services. Gradual fusion would inevitably be sensitive, primarily for the officer corps in the early stages, but politicians occasionally tend to underestimate the common professional interests of military men, especially those with a shared nationality.

It is, however, the longer term German problem of the potential superpower which is prompting the greater debate. And here I must confess to a minority, rather optimistic, view. I can fully understand the concern of my continental friends whose memories of German militarism are personal and painful. Nineteen-ninety is, after all, the fiftieth anniversary of the Battle of Britain. Nor has Chancellor Kohl always been as sensitive or diplomatic in recent months as he might have been. A unified Germany would undoubtedly become the strongest economic and political power in Central Europe, and it might decide to buttress that power with military strength appropriate to its status. Indeed, it might seek to include nuclear weaponry in its armory and it might set out for the third time in a century to unite all German-speaking peoples under one regime. That is an apocalyptic scenario. There are three reasons, before even considering some kind of constraining security arrangement, why I believe it to be unlikely.

The first is that West Germany, which will dominate German domestic and foreign policy decisions for the foreseeable future, has now had 45 years experience, shared with the West, of economic and political cooperation based on a stable and widely respected democratic framework. Those elements have induced unprecedented prosperity and a justifiable self-confidence which shows no inclination towards militarism: indeed, just the opposite. The second reason for optimism lies, paradoxically, in a forecast prompting unease among some European observers. The East German provinces will be early beneficiaries of West German wealth, although perhaps not to the levels or at the speed of current expectations. Thereafter the new Germany will play an increasingly influential economic role in Central Europe and eastern Europe, either independently or as part of an extended western European economic and political structure. Such economic interests will thrive best on stability and cooperation. Arrogant militarism would be destabilizing and counterproductive.

My third reason for optimism is that there is another folk memory in Europe about German militarism, that held by the Germans themselves, of the retribution wreaked on Germany in World War II. It is unquantifiable and only of historical record to the modern generation, but if we are to take into account the unease of the Third Reich's victims' successors, we cannot discount a residual German awareness of the likely consequences of a third attempt to impose German hegemony on Europe. What combination of western malaise, Soviet indifference, and U.S. disinterest must we envisage to construct a scenario of a Fourth Reich? Boundary disputes are one thing, but a quest for *Lebensraum*, again?

In sum, I believe we must not reach for an artificial security system which by its fears of and constraints on Germany could encourage the very symptoms it is designed to forestall.

But regardless of the pessimism or otherwise of our forecasts about the future inclinations of a unified Germany, there remain the sources of instability within and between the other countries now freed from Soviet domination. Among them there is no history of peaceful conciliation, no common political bond, and no obvious counterpoise of economic complementary cooperation. The only shared interests of the non-Soviet Warsaw Pact states are a rejection of communism and hostility to Soviet military occupation. As the Russian tide recedes, familiar landmarks reappear with disputed boundaries and ethnic minorities prominent among them.

Again, however, the potential for infectious instability should not be exaggerated. I use the world "infectious" advisedly, and would cite the current example of Yugoslavia, where ethnic unrest and potential political disintegration are more threatening than at any time since 1948. For many years precisely these circumstances were feared as a catalyst for East-West confrontation and figured prominently in military staff college scenarios. I have seen no signs of intervention by any other powers and no moves toward escalation; indeed, I do not recall seeing Yugoslavia mentioned in any recent East-West deliberations. It is the circumstances of Yugoslavia in 1990 rather than Sarajevo in 1914 which more realistically indicate the scale of instability to be expected in eastern Europe. No great power has any foreseeable interest in either fomenting or aggravating border or ethnic disputes. One can foresee an uneasy Soviet Union or a sensitive Germany protective of related minorities, but not disputes provoking large-scale military intervention by a third party. The need will much more likely be for a cooperative security organization capable of dispatching peacekeeping forces on a scale similar to those of the United Nations in Cyprus or Sinai.

These assumptions confirm the popular conclusions that future threats to European security are likely to come most seriously from a weakened, demoralized but unpredictable Soviet Union with considerable residual military strength, possibly from a unified Germany which would have learned nothing and remembered nothing from her last seventy-five years, and on a much smaller scale from isolated and unrelated incidents in an eastern Europe bereft of cooperative example and democratic experience.

In parentheses I emphasize that I have no doubts about Mr. Gorbachev's desire to concentrate his efforts on restructuring his crumbling empire, to reconfigure his armed forces, to abjure if at all possible the use of force in Europe. Nor do I expect a military coup in Moscow and a surge to reassert Soviet hegemony in a desperate attempt to preserve the ancien regime in the Soviet Union. It is simply that a combination of political instability, economic bankruptcy, imperial disintegration, ideological despair, and access to large stocks of conventional, nuclear, and chemical weapons comprise a very combustible compound.

Nevertheless, the Soviet Union, the United States, Britain, and France will retain international interests beyond Europe. Whatever the European security framework they are likely to wish to retain a potential for influence.

European Security Requirements

What then are the security requirements prompted by these assumptions? We must recognize the potential contradictions in the requirements. We need to provide for the eventuality of the Soviet Union being responsible for instability, while at the same time incorporating it in a security system. If we fear the destabilizing potential of a greater Germany, we need to establish military constraints which it will not only voluntarily accept but which will not inhibit it from playing a proportionate role in the system itself. Compared with those two contradictions, resolution of minor squabbles or even national conflict between eastern European states is placed firmly into perspective.

The first requirement is a consultative forum which hopefully will resolve disputes before they provoke open conflict. There seems to be an unspoken consensus that this is a European and North Atlantic regional affair and not therefore the concern of the United Nations. If so, the Conference on Security and Cooperation in Europe (CSCE) could be the foundation of such a forum. Given a modest permanent organization, it could also meet the second requirement: maintenance of a peacekeeping force as required to facilitate resolution of disputes in eastern Europe until such time as habits of political compromise and economic cooperation come to be nurtured. In the short term the use of hitherto neutral forces, for example Swedes, Finns, Austrians, Irish, Yugoslavs, and Swiss in a peacekeeping intervention role would be likely to be more politically acceptable to both the recipients and a still sensitive Soviet Union, albeit the traditional Swiss interpretation of its neutrality would require redefinition. At present, any action by the CSCE requires a unanimous vote. Either that principle would require amendment, or it would need to be disregarded. In either case it is obvious that the CSCE could never prepare, initiate, and coordinate large-scale military action against a major European power. The role of the CSCE, therefore, should be as a European consultative assembly with power to authorize and maintain designated peacekeeping forces drawn initially at least from countries with no previous association with the existing major alliances.

The third requirement is a security system strong enough to discourage and if ultimately necessary contain a wayward

Soviet Union. It is the ingredient which would preserve a balance of power across the reconstructed map of Europe. It is already in position and functioning. It is NATO which has represented the security aspirations of the Atlantic community for over forty years. The aspirations have not changed, simply the nature and extent of the threat. The original articles of the treaty are still valid: "to consult together whenever the territorial integrity, political independence or security of any member is threatened . . . to take such action as is deemed necessary to restore and maintain the integrity of the Atlantic area."

Nevertheless, if NATO is not to become an anachronism, and even more important in the time of rising expectations of peace dividends, if it is not to be perceived as an anachronism, it must be prepared to adjust to changed circumstances. In an ideal world the alliance would have the time and collective will to coordinate a two-stage progression.

The first would be the restructuring prompted solely by the CFE process which will require an overall reduction of approximately 15 percent in the specified items and the construction of a verification regime. That could occupy NATO military staffs very productively for the next two or three years and reductions on such a scale would not call for any significant adjustment to current NATO military strategy or organization. The product would be a well-balanced international force whose members had agreed on proportionate and strategically complementary national reductions, divested themselves of obsolescent equipment, avoided multinational procurement pressures, put the common good of the alliance ahead of national interests, and emerged from the process well prepared to negotiate a further second stage of force reductions and adjustment to the new European political landscape.

Unless there is a dramatic and unwelcome change in Soviet activities, the alliance will in practice have no such unimpeded opportunity. Implementation of CFE agreements will have to take place at the same time as other, more fundamental readjustments prompted by the need to accommodate the new Germany, meet the widespread western expectations of a peace dividend, while at the same time maintaining adequate military insurance against residual Soviet military capability.

The desired end product is relatively easy to define; identification of the constituent steps is much more difficult.

The end product would be an alliance in which American military presence on the ground in Europe would be considerably reduced but the Atlantic commitment preserved. Further possible bilateral agreements between NATO and the Soviet Union would reduce all conventional forces in Europe below the current CFE levels with reductions concentrated on the central regions occupied by the two Germanies. Reduction of U.S. forces in Europe would be matched by a reduction in U.S. representation at senior command level, thereby encouraging a revision of recent French attitudes toward the military structure.

Further reduced force levels on both sides, the erasure of the inner German border, the disintegration of the Warsaw Pact, and a verified major reconstruction of Soviet forces and associated doctrine will prompt a reevaluation of the armed forces required to underpin a revised Atlantic alliance. The preservation of territorial integrity of NATO members will remain a major reason for alliance participation, and this interest argues against the view that the alliance should readily shed commitments to forward defense, even when the forward frontier becomes the Oder-Neisse line.

The nature of the provision for that defense can undoubtedly be changed. In the scenario envisaged, post-CFE verification measures would involve monitoring Soviet force deployments, readiness states, and the output of procurement programs. Soviet ground forces would be present in eastern Europe in much smaller numbers if at all, and no other eastern nation would have the military capacity to threaten a NATO member unilaterally. Warning time of a major incursion, requiring at least partial Soviet mobilization and the transport of forces across eastern Europe, would be measured in weeks rather than days. Only an air attack, and possibly airborne assault, could hope to achieve any degree of surprise.

Under those circumstances there would be no military requirement for a new generation of Lance nuclear weapons, because there would be no overwhelming Soviet ground force numerical superiority to counter, quite apart from any political considerations of popular opposition to the development of new nuclear weapons. The movement of Soviet ground forces across eastern Europe would either be by agreement—in which case we have created a very different set of assumptions—or by violating neutrality and risking national opposition almost certainly supported by NATO probably in the form of deep air strikes. By definition, the intermediate airspace between NATO territory and Soviet advanced positions would lack hostile ground to air defenses. Aircraft with such a deep offensive capability would, because of the warning times involved, not require peacetime basing in Central Europe, as long as forward operating bases were available in crisis or transition to war. Consequently, forward defense in peacetime could rest on highly mobile helicopter transportable ground forces, reduced proportions of heavy armor, a tactical air element, a flexible mix of ground and air-to-air defensive systems, and comprehensive surveillance and airborne early warning. Such a force mix would allow the reduction of regular forces, reduction in periods of conscript service, and greater use of reserves and auxiliaries. A shift of emphasis from offensive to defensive counter air operations would be militarily feasible and politically constructive. The combination of reduction in forces and overall shift of emphasis would enhance the political acceptability of maintaining foreign forces in Germany, particularly if they were constituted multinationally as proposed by the British government. Such proposals are necessarily tentative and generalized, because they are the end product of deductions from both basic assumptions and as yet uncertain developments.

We should distinguish clearly between specific weapons systems, e.g., a new Lance missile—and the retention in Europe of a substrategic nuclear capability. The Soviet Union will remain a nuclear power and indeed may be moving towards a posture of minimal nuclear deterrence. The political significance—as opposed to a warfighting potential of nuclear weapons—will remain. In view of proliferation in the third world they may well come to assume an out of area significance also. I therefore envisage a modernized, stand-off air-launched set of nuclear weapon systems by the United States, United Kingdom, and France with a collective alliance endorsement of the theater nuclear link in a flexible response chain, but with reduced numbers of weapons and delivery systems. There would be no military requirement for delivery systems to be based in peacetime in every allied country, but the principle of risk sharing should be endorsed by a principle of acceptance of forward basing in times of tension or transition to war.

The preservation of an Atlantic alliance is not incompatible with either perceptions of a reduced Soviet threat, nor the creation of an overarching, Helsinki derived, European framework. The alliance could be sustained with considerably reduced national contributions. It would ensure that whatever instability or unpredictable events occurred to the East a stable, cooperative security base remained for the benefit of its current membership.

With reduced forces and a revised defensive forward strategy which incorporated German forces in an integrated military structure, lingering fears in eastern Europe and the Soviet Union would be assuaged. As long as nuclear weapons remained in national inventories, maintaining a mobile, tightly controlled theater nuclear deterrent endorsed by all members but remaining in American, British, and French hands would ensure the preservation of the transatlantic linkage.

In sum, a future European security system should build progressively on existing structures. CSCE should be transformed into a permanent, or regularly constituted assembly, to oversee all security issues. Members hitherto neutral in the East-West confrontation should be encouraged and funded via CSCE to contribute to peacekeeping operations as required in eastern Europe. Just as Article 51 of the United Nations Charter recognized the utility of regional defensive groupings, so the continued existence of the NATO alliance would not be incompatible with the new CSCE organization. NATO strategy and force levels should, however, be reconfigured along the lines suggested. The CSCE could be expanded in a very short time frame of months, provided that the peacekeeping proposals proved acceptable. The possibility of major reconstruction of NATO deployments and strategy should be swiftly acknowledged and widely publicized, but its practical implementation should be carefully staged to ensure that no irretrievable, untimely steps are taken. Progressive measures, providing progressive peace dividends are likely to produce more lasting, stable, and cooperative security in Europe than an attempt to create a comprehensive system based in temporary circumstances and fearful shadows from the past.

Chapter 10

Implications of German Unification for European Security

Viktor Shein

The situation we face now in Europe is not only completely different as compared with what we had just a year ago, but it still continues to evolve. And this is obviously an evolution in one main direction—toward a final termination of the post–World War II period of European history. Although the next period of this history has not yet formally begun, the majority of experts in the Soviet Union, and I believe in other countries as well, have practically no doubts that the decisive step along this road is already inevitable and this will be unification of the two German states.

Even though changes of such magnitude are on balance absolutely legitimate and positive, it is natural that they nevertheless create a number of problems. For example, they have become a source of anxiety for ordinary people and whole countries about the prospects of solid peace and security in Europe. In any case, it is evident that the decisions on Germany being taken or planned demand a huge sense of responsibility since they could launch irreversible processes.

At the present time the discussion in the West and to a certain extent in the East is mainly focused on the idea of including a unified Germany in the North Atlantic Treaty Organization (NATO). This idea has already found strong support almost everywhere except the Soviet Union. This support can at least partly be explained by the emotional strength of the basic argument which holds that Germany has to be bound to western structures, to be "kept down," or otherwise it would become a factor detrimental to the stability of Europe.

Such arguments based on emotions or aimed to raise emotions look fine at first glance. Even for some Soviets they could appear to be convincing and intellectually understandable. Nobody really wants to have in Europe a Germany that is unpredictable, nationalistic, and—what is obviously implied—ambitious in a negative sense.

But putting emotions aside, one cannot avoid asking several questions. Why should all this necessarily happen with Germany being out of NATO? Why apply to the future only worst-case scenarios? Is there any reliable information which could confirm the correctness of this tendency on the part of a united Germany? If such danger exists, what can NATO practically do to prevent it?

In my view many of the speculations and anxieties concerning the future of a united Germany are not totally valid. Is Germany going to cease to exist as a democratic country? Is membership in NATO the only way to keep it democratic? For me, the answer to both questions is "no."

There is yet another aspect of the same problem. Suppose for a moment that at a later stage the United States takes a decision to implement its traditional threat to withdraw from NATO and Europe in some way. Theoretically such a situation is possible. Then, given that NATO would still exist as a military alliance, Germany could have the power to dominate Europe not only economically and politically, but militarily as well. One must seriously doubt that such an event would make other Europeans very happy. Certainly an outcome of this sort is highly unlikely. But to speak about such a development is not demonstrably more or less likely than to predict a nationalistic nonallied Germany ready to force its influence on other countries.

Goals of U.S. Policy

This leads me to note that there are other reasons behind the United States' position that are clearly motivated by factors other than the intention to control Germany. One can identify such goals as saving NATO from the collapse which is believed possible without Germany as a central participant, keeping the more and more integrated Europe anchored in the wider Atlantic structure, and not allowing Germany to exploit its theoretical option of rapprochement with the Soviet Union.

If all these goals are practically justified, the insistence on Germany's inclusion in NATO can at least be regarded as serious. But are they?

I believe that the survival of NATO does depend on German participation, but only to a marginal degree. Moreover, the western alliance could pass away with Germany in or continue to function with Germany out. Everything will depend on new circumstances and on the ability of the NATO politicians to manage them.

To my understanding the western alliance in its current form is undergoing real difficulties, because the situation has so drastically changed. Until recently many NATO supporters and officials had been satisfied and were not worried about the future. Military confrontation with the Warsaw Pact kept NATO alive and healthy. Now the situation is entirely different not only in the Soviet Union and eastern Europe, but also in U.S.–West European relations. This new situation makes politicians reconsider both the value and orientation of NATO. Several factors work together to demand new thinking in the West:

- The development of the European Community creates the prospect of growing political and economic competition between the United States and western Europe. As a result the importance of NATO appears to be declining for both America and its allies.
- The deepening of all-European cooperation and progress in arms control undermines the role of military security issues as a factor of strengthening NATO and American–West European solidarity.
- The revolutions in eastern Europe along with arms control have already resulted in changes in the nature of the Warsaw Pact which can hardly be considered anymore a traditional rival justifying NATO's existence.
- Most important, NATO has proved to be unable to contain the unification of Germany, a task that has always been considered vital though unofficial. With unification becom-

ing a fact of life, the aim of extending NATO's control over Germany, doubtful from the political point of view, loses its practical significance. It appears unlikely that the previous situation can be restored, even with full German participation.

The principal problems for NATO are those of age and evolving environment. In such circumstances a unified Germany within NATO is certainly not the best medicine. On the other hand, the illness does not seem to be mortal and just demands radical measures of readjustment to the outside and inside changes. In my view NATO can survive without Germany. But it is much less likely that the alliance could be modernized along nonmilitary lines with a unified Germany as a full member. This means that the aim of keeping NATO going could simply become unattainable.

As to the other two aims mentioned earlier—retaining an integrated Europe in the broader Atlantic structure and preventing Germany's drift in the direction of the Soviet Union— these goals do not make very much sense. The U.S.–European Community relationship has outgrown existing patterns, and the development of new tactics, strategies, and mechanisms is already on the agenda. The scope and content of any increased cooperation between Germany and the Soviet Union will in any case mostly depend not on NATO, but on German participation in the European Community and on creating favorable preconditions including first of all the reform of the Soviet economy. Therefore, I contend that a unified Germany in NATO may not be the best solution even from the point of view of western interests.

Soviet Concerns and Policy Objectives

I would like to introduce some additional arguments from the Soviet perspective to support my position. First, a united Germany's participation in NATO could push events toward creating in Europe a superstructure with a possibility of including still other countries but with no place for the Soviet Union. This would amount to an exclusion of the Soviet Union from Europe, even if there were other less meaningful multilateral institutions. Such an outcome could neither please the Soviet Union, nor contribute to the stability of Europe as a whole. The only option for the Soviet Union would be to go it alone at a time when European developments could be perceived in Moscow as threatening its security and other vital interests. In present circumstances it is not possible to predict what kind of impact such a result would produce on events in the Soviet Union. At least from modern history it is clear that no nation in a corner feels like unilaterally disarming or restraining itself from geopolitical steps necessary to secure its interests.

Second, no one should ignore the fact that a unified Germany in NATO would produce an extremely unfavorable impression in the Soviet Union. The majority of the population would react in a negative way. Even the idea of unification itself has provoked sharp debates at all levels. If a unified Germany becomes a member of NATO, this will result in a wave of criticism of Soviet foreign policy. Candidly, this would be a most unwelcome development in light of the complexities of the Soviet internal situation as well as the obvious intention of the leadership to rely upon our foreign policy achievements in order to justify the importance of further reductions in military spending, reform of defense doctrine, force withdrawals, and arms control agreements.

Third, almost all current debate focuses on only two options: Germany inside or outside of NATO. This approach might be simplistic, especially if you take into account that unification has not yet occurred and no one knows when it is going to happen. Most likely it will take years, and it has recently slowed down when faced with many serious problems. By the time full unification becomes a reality, Europeans and Americans can have created other structures based on new ideas. In any event, the question of German participation in NATO does not demand a definite answer today or tomorrow.

On balance, it seems to me that the Soviet stance on the German situation as on events in Europe as a whole is dominated by moderation and pragmatism. Western states should encourage this policy to continue and should shape their policy to achieve the best results for all nations involved, not just base their actions on a limited number of worst-case scenarios. In particular, one should appreciate that forthcoming arms control decisions will allow substantially reduced conventional armed forces and will move toward working out further measures of military build-down. We should realize that multilateral cooperation is going to play a more important role in Europe, that increasing Soviet-American contacts and continued U.S. involvement in European affairs could help create a climate necessary for strengthening mutual trust, and that the countries belonging to the European Community will take care of maintaining good relations with the countries of the eastern bloc both before and after 1992.

In sum, all these and some other factors of the same nature could make it possible for Europeans to move away gradually from the current political order and security system which are built on the military alliances. The alternative could be a new system based mainly on nonmilitary structures and factors, on confidence and cooperation, and designed for all countries and open to any of them.

Examining the problem of German unification from this broader angle of view, one will see the importance of coordination between the process of unification and the general integrating trend in Europe. This conclusion seems to be fairly reasonable, especially in light of the prospect for the deepening of integration, the possibility of adoption by the end of this year of some multilateral decisions dealing with aspects of unification, and the good chance that the process of German unification may take more time than was previously expected.

Role of the CSCE

In thinking of a new system of security for Europe, it is my conviction that the Conference on Security and Cooperation in Europe (CSCE) is the only way to provide a substitute for the current obsolete bloc system. Are there any other options? Theoretically, there are two others. One of them was described above: NATO plus Germany with the Soviet Union being an outsider. This option is totally unacceptable for the Soviet Union. The second option also appears to me somewhat unrealistic. It is a three-pillar system: the United States, Europe, the Soviet Union. This option could only be realized in the event that America and the Soviet Union decide to withdraw from Europe, an outcome that is highly unlikely. Such a result would not be in the interests of Europe, given the interdependence of the world and the abundance of acute global and other problems which can only be overcome through the cooperative action of all major countries or groups of countries.

Thus the CSCE remains the only reasonable and promising basis on which a new all-European system of security and cooperation can be established. In my view the importance of the Helsinki process has been underestimated in the West, especially in the United States. The situation with the Soviet Union and eastern Europe is a different one. These countries have felt the influence of the CSCE since its very beginning. It was one of the main factors, for example, which helped the Soviet Union to start radical political and economic reforms. Being at least partly responsible for the revolutions in this part of Europe, the CSCE process is in the best position to cement the results of these revolutions and to contribute to safeguarding stability in Europe.

Certainly there are serious questions about what can practically be done to adjust the present ad hoc process to new tasks and demands. My impression is that a basic consensus is forming on what is needed to institutionalize the CSCE. The sooner agreement is reached the better. The meeting of the heads of the CSCE countries in late 1990 could launch some initiatives of this kind and further steps could be taken at the next Helsinki summit meeting to be held in 1992. Most specialists and officials agree that these proposals should include the creation of a permanent CSCE structure including a mechanism that can help implement and verify the results of arms control agreements. I would like to emphasize that an expansion and institutionalization of the CSCE does not mean automatic elimination of the structures that already exist in Europe. NATO and perhaps the Warsaw Pact as well as the West European Union could become important contributors to the creation of an all-European security system. The Council of Europe could also join this framework, creating still more possibilities for dialogue and cooperation.*

*Editor's Note: The Soviet Union firmly maintained the posture, reflected in Viktor Shein's essay, of opposition to a unified Germany being a member of NATO through the May 30–June 3, 1990, Bush-Gorbachev summit in

Washington. But by the end of the first week of June 1990 there were signs from the June 5 talks between U.S. Secretary of State James Baker and Soviet Foreign Minister Eduard Shevardnadze that a compromise might be worked out through the device of an agreement between NATO and the Warsaw Pact. See John M. Goshko and Glenn Frankel, ''NATO Ministers Hopeful on Germany,'' *Washington Post*, June 8, 1990, p. 30, and Michael Dobbs, ''Warsaw Pact Summit Urges Transformation,'' *Washington Post*, June 8, 1990, p. 25.

By July 16, as a result of the assurances conveyed from the NATO summit in London and extensive talks with Helmut Kohl and Hans-Dietrich Genscher, the Soviet leadership abandoned its opposition to a unified Germany belonging to NATO. See Serge Schmemann, ''Gorbachev Clears Way for German Unity, Dropping Objection to NATO Membership,'' *New York Times*, July 17, 1990, p. 1.

Chapter 11

The Challenges to European Security: A Polish View

Bronisław Geremek

I am optimistic but not unrealistic about the situation in Central Europe. Anything is possible, including the fact that Poland, Czechoslovakia, and Hungary might revert back to a communist system. But there is strong evidence that this is unlikely and that the changes in Central Europe and the Soviet Union are irreversible. And I have a feeling that the Central European revolutions, and perhaps most of all the Polish revolution, matter for the future of Europe and for the future of the world.

The future of world security holds three major problems: the German, the Russian, and the Central European. The German question is not an issue of the Oder-Neisse border; this is not open for debate, as everyone knows. I was in Lithuania recently and thought it my duty to tell Lithuanians that Poland accepts the current borders because sometimes I feel that western observers are not aware of the fact that in 1945 Reich Germany ceded approximately one-third of Polish territory to the Soviet Union, Lithuania, Belorussia, and the Ukraine. I told the Lithuanians that I have no problem with the Polish-Lithuanian border and that I expected the same kind of free, frank speech from Germany. I am aware that the Oder-Neisse frontier is accepted by a majority of West German public opinion and that there is a consensus among Germans with regard to this. But is it a consensus with all but one, the West German Chancellor?

In the last few days I have been asked several times about the prospects for a treaty guaranteeing the border between Poland and a unified Germany and about the preconditions asked by West German Chancellor Kohl. My answer is that I cannot understand why the German government has rejected the Polish proposal for a treaty recognizing the Oder-Neisse line as the permanent border between Poland and Germany to be ratified by the parliament of the new unified Germany. I regret the fact that the border has been used for domestic political reasons and hope that a solution will be found that can address the sensitivities on both sides.

My reaction to the three preconditions demanded by Chancellor Kohl is more complicated. He has asked for: a) renunciation of all demands for indemnities (state and individual) by Poland, b) an apology by the Polish government for all the hardships endured by the German population during and after World War II, and c) measures to protect the rights of the German minority in Poland. I contend the question of indemnities can be settled through negotiations. On the issue of the apology I would not have any problem apologizing to the German victims of hardship, but I will never do it because it is demanded by a German politician who is toying with national emotions. With regard to the German minority in Poland, I would point out that two other minorities are substantially larger in number than the German and all of these minority groups in Poland enjoy a wide range of rights and protection.

I should emphasize that not only do Poles accept German unification, they are happy about it. The division of Germany was the result of a political argument emphasizing the special role of the Soviet Union, and the Poles did not like it. German unification is the realization of the right of self-determination which each people has. But it would be far better for the United States, Europe, and Germany if this question of borders were not treated as part of a political game, in which the ruling party, the Christian Democratic Union, is seeking to win an additional 2 percent of public support in the next elections. I believe that the question of borders should be out of the political game and should not be considered as an instrument toward political ends, and I hope that a clearer declaration regarding borders will come. This development will mean that the German political leadership understands not only the chance which unification gives to the world but also the dangers which can be connected with unification.

The power and position of the German economy assures us of the western orientation of the new European superpower. West Germany is a democratic state, a fact it has proven time and time again. But it is also true that there exists in East Germany a Nazi past that has not been fully acknowledged and dealt with and this, along with Russian nationalistic feelings, creates the possibility of the revival of very old ghosts. The situation can be changed. A very clear response is necessary vis-à-vis European security and the question of borders.

When I state that there are real problems in the world such as the German and the Soviet, the first response I get is: ''This is your Polish problem and headache.'' But this is not just a concern for Poland. The Soviet problem is related to the future of the Soviet Union, and this is very important for the world. When we view the collapse of communist ideology and of Soviet rule in Central Europe as the proof that one only has to wait for the demise of the Soviet Union, this is not the way to aid perestroika. Thinking this way is wrong; the Soviet Union still remains a superpower. The real question is: does the collapse of the Soviet empire reflect the beginning of a change inside the Soviet Union itself? Andrei Sakharov, in the months before his death, said that the future of the Soviet Union depends largely on its capacity to abandon its imperial structures and become a federation. If perestroika and the philosophy of action existing today in the Soviet Union collapses, the world could face great danger. Nuclear weapons are still available to potential leaders in Moscow, and no one knows what the future will hold for the Soviet Union.

The events of 1989 in Central Europe gave tremendous hope to the world. It was a year of freedom in Central Europe, and should not be considered simply as a victory of one superpower over another. It was a victory of values and the human spirit, and it demonstrated society's resistance to an oppressive regime. But now this hope which Central Europe brought to the world faces dangers itself, and this poses a threat to the future political architecture of Europe. Central Europe is unleashing national and ethnic problems that can give a new headache to Europe and the world. There are nationality problems in Yugoslavia, the issue of Hungarian minorities in Romania, and in Slovakia, and many others.

How will the world respond to these changes? The Helsinki process can help with an answer. But the actual situation today finds little basis for assistance, because the Conference on Security and Cooperation in Europe (CSCE) process is a series of conferences, not a structure. Up to now officials and specialists have advanced many proposals for the CSCE process, but no action has been taken that can offer early help. Perhaps the Council of Europe is the structure that can answer the needs of the moment. Poland, Czechoslovakia, and Hungary have applied for membership in the Council of Europe, but they are still waiting for an answer. There are no reasons to wait. These are three democratic countries that have committed themselves to market economies and basic human rights, and still they are waiting for a response. I can understand why the European Community cannot respond immediately to the desire of the weak and economically poor countries of Central Europe to join the Community. But why do we still wait for an answer from the Council of Europe?

Another important issue concerns the future presence of the United States and the Soviet Union in the new political architecture of Europe. The CSCE process offers a good framework because both superpowers are engaged, but more is needed. The idea of a common European home and the concept of the European confederation both express to a degree the expectation that the United States' role in Europe will diminish. Such a result is neither in the interest of Europe, nor in the interest of the United States. The history of the twentieth century should teach Europeans a lesson about the desirability, even necessity, of a continued United States presence on the European scene. It would be the irony of history if as a result of the high hopes of 1989 the Soviet Union obtained a presence in the political architecture of Europe while the United States lost its position. I find it profoundly disturbing that it is the West Europeans who are raising this prospect!

The Central European countries need to know how western nations will help them maintain their revolutions. The answer should be both political and economic. In many ways the economic aspects are more important, because the economic reforms in Poland and other countries are the main issue of the democratic process. One can even say that the future of the democratic process depends on the success of the economic reform process. What we have now in Central Europe is not democracy but freedom, and freedom by itself does not guarantee democracy. Freedom for Central European peoples in the midst of a difficult material situation could result in the return of another authoritarian regime, which would represent a severe defeat for democracy. In this sense the future of the Central European democracies depends on the success of economic reforms which began in Poland first and which will take place in Hungary, Czechoslovakia, the Soviet Union, and other parts of eastern Europe.

Many questions remain open about how the western world will respond to this new challenge. Will it be with a sense of victory? Will the western world simply rejoice that it won in its struggle between two superpowers, systems, and ideologies? This kind of triumphalism could have very negative results. How will the western world answer first the economic aspirations and needs of Central Europe, and then the political aspirations, for a place in the European integration process? Finally, how will Europe and the world answer the need not only for stability but also for security for Central European countries?

Chapter 12

The U.S. Role in European Security

Philip D. Zelikow

What is the overall objective of U.S. foreign policy for Europe during the next two years? Perhaps the best description of that overall goal came from President Bush in a meeting with the Irish Prime Minister, Charles Haughey, when he was here as the President of the European Community. After lunch everyone was in a jovial mood, and the Prime Minister told the President he was doing a terrific job, giving an impeccable performance, and that American foreign policy was in great shape. The President thanked him and said that his basic guideline was borrowed from the baseball philosopher Yogi Berra. After a game that his Yankees won Berra was asked the secret of his success, and he replied: "We didn't make the wrong mistakes!" This captures it rather well for the Bush administration. We are in a very turbulent period in European politics, an extremely challenging period for American foreign policy, and we are bound to make some mistakes in navigating through these difficult waters. The big watchword for us is not to make the wrong mistakes. Within this very practical context, let me try to assess the present environment for European security and alliance relationships and look a bit into the future.

We are living today through a period of dramatic upheaval in European politics. If you look back on the record of American foreign policy, you will find that in the aftermath of any period of extreme change in European politics the leadership of the United States is called upon to make fundamental choices about the role of America in European affairs. We are now living through the fifth such period in American history.

The first one was the period immediately after the French Revolution and proceeding through its Napoleonic aftermath. The second was during the period from 1914 to 1920 when America had to make fundamental decisions about its participation in the first World War and in the peace settlement that followed it. The third was in the period from 1934 to 1941 when, faced with dramatic upheaval in Europe and the rise of the totalitarian powers, the United States had to make basic choices about its involvement in European politics. And the fourth period was from 1941 to 1951, when most of the major choices America was going to make about its postwar goals and its postwar relationship to Europe were put in place.

We are now in the fifth such period of change, and important choices are before the United States. If, as many contend, the rationale for our postwar military and political involvement in Europe is expiring, then we must seriously reflect on the fundamental bases for American interests in Europe. We should not take it for granted that because we have been successful so far in the postwar period we can assume that the American people will continue to support our overseas commitment without significant change. If we believe that aspects of this commitment should continue, we have to be prepared to make the case for doing so.

To Remain a European Power

The first choice for the United States is to determine its basic role in Europe. During these interesting times ahead, the United States intends to remain a European power, as the President declared at the end of November last year. This involves being a European power in all of the dimensions of that term—political, military, and economic. The administration intends for our commitment to be balanced among all these dimensions; we cannot concentrate simply on a military commitment to Europe at the expense of our parallel political and economic obligations. The United States must be in a position to be influential in European affairs both to maintain our own interests and to be able to play the appropriate role in the evolution of the new Europe.

This statement of broad policy objectives contains implications for the kinds of institutions we want to see arise in Europe and the American involvement in those institutions. We do not think the United States' involvement in Europe is a charitable donation; we have thought for some time that it is very much in America's interest to remain as a European power. Postwar history has demonstrated that upheaval in Europe inevitably affects vital American interests and that the United States must act in times of peace to protect its interests—political, military, and economic—because its fate is linked inseparably to the fate of Europe.

The United States' relationship with Europe is very much a two-way street. With America pledging that its fate is inextricably tied to that of Europe, Europe for its part must accept that America will have a role in its affairs and influence in the political, military, and economic dimensions of its activities. That is a very important statement about European politics, and it goes well beyond the idea that we need better burden sharing in our common defense. While the burden sharing point may be true, we are making a much broader statement about an American voice in European affairs.

During the important period of change ahead, the North Atlantic Treaty Organization (NATO) is the primary vehicle for the American commitment in Europe. There are no other institutions that could be sold to the American people as offering the same legitimacy, the same international authority, and the same viability for the U.S. commitment in Europe. Let us look for a moment at the nature of that commitment. When the North Atlantic alliance was actually negotiated, it was not intended to include a significant American military presence in Europe. The Truman administration contended that the United States was making through this treaty a fundamental political statement about our country's relationship to Europe. The military commitments followed later, based on decisions that were made principally in 1950 and 1951 after the outbreak of the Korean War, and they represented an extension under new and threatening circumstances of the political commitment that had been made in the North Atlantic Treaty itself.

Robert Lovett, one of the great American statesmen of the postwar period who, as Marshall's Under Secretary of State in 1948, was the leader of our negotiating team when the North Atlantic Treaty was being negotiated. He said in 1948 that, after many heartbreaks, America had decided that it was going to be involved in Europe, and now all that remained was to decide what would be the proof of our determination. This remains the essential question, and I believe the answer is going to be that the American presence in Europe needs to remain very strong and it needs to have an active military component. Therefore the United States will retain militarily significant forces in Europe for the foreseeable future. Thus our involvement in Europe includes the underlying political compact that derives from the North Atlantic Treaty as well as the subsequently determined military commitment.

Let me comment briefly on Senator Sam Nunn's statements about the extent of the American presence in Europe. Senator Nunn is billed as having disagreed with the administration in saying that the President's proposal for a minimum of 195,000 troops in Europe in the mid-1990s is excessive. I do not want to quarrel here over exactly what our force structure should be in Europe. But you do create a problem when you say on the one hand, as Senator Nunn did, that we should rely on a conventional arms control process to coordinate in a stabilizing way the nature of both sides' troop commitments in Europe, and then say, on the other hand, that we should disregard our Conventional Forces in Europe (CFE) position and unilaterally go down to a lower force level. We would be much more comfortable with a position that said, after we have negotiated a CFE treaty and implemented it and after the Soviet Union has withdrawn from eastern Europe, we will take a hard look at the situation and determine what should be the U.S. force presence. Senator Nunn's speeches are an important contribution to the debate on U.S. policy. The essential point now, though, is that the United States must retain a militarily significant commitment of its forces in Europe as evidence of its determination politically to stay involved in protecting the stability of the European continent.

European Security Architecture

What does this discussion of the U.S. role in Europe imply for the design of European security architecture? The first point to make is the absolute centrality of the future of Germany to all concepts of European architecture. As the President has said on several occasions, the United States welcomes the realization of German unification in peace and freedom, a goal we have sought for all these decades. The President has given his unambiguous support for the realization of that objective and if it is happening faster than we had originally planned, so much the better. Further, if Germany is unified, as now appears to be the case, in a peaceful fashion with viable democratic institutions, we believe that such a unified Germany should have its full sovereignty restored. We look to the "two plus four" process that is now negotiating the external aspects of the establishment of German unity to focus principally on how to devolve the special four-power rights and responsibilities that were the legacy of the wartime and postwar agreements and return full sovereign authority to a united German state.

On the issue of Germany's relationship to NATO, I am afraid I will have to disagree with our Soviet colleague who makes an interesting argument that I have not previously heard. We have said for some time that if the Soviets looked at this issue carefully, they would see that German membership in NATO is genuinely in the Soviet interest. Mr. Shein (Chapter 10) now turns this argument precisely around—he says that if we really thought about it, we would realize that a Germany out of NATO is really in the American interest, and that German membership in NATO is marginal to NATO's health, in any event. My response to that would be to quote one of my favorite characters from Hemingway, Jake Barnes, in that immortal concluding line from *The Sun Also Rises*: "Isn't it pretty to think so?"

We believe that German membership in NATO is absolutely indispensable to NATO's health. In fact, I will go on to assert that if a united Germany is not a member of NATO, a lot of the questions we are currently debating about finding a new political role for NATO will be rendered moot and basically irrelevant because NATO will have been dealt a mortal blow.

The United States would like for NATO to play a larger political role in the new Europe. The most important political role for NATO is to function as an agent of change in Europe rather than be perceived as than an anachronistic institution of the past. This does not mean that we have to embark on a major restructuring of the North Atlantic alliance. There is no crisis in NATO; it has worked very successfully; and what it needs is not drastic reform but steady evolution to meet the needs of a new situation. The key to steady evolution is to make it clear to European publics that NATO is part of the American role in Europe, and proposals such as replacing an

American Supreme Allied Commander with a French general do not help in this effort. If the need is to reassure Europeans that the United States will maintain its basic commitment to Europe, we would be sending a somewhat inconsistent signal by abandoning one of the major symbols of the American commitment to Europe at this particular time.

Going beyond NATO's political role, we should examine a third facet of the new European architecture, the question of military requirements. This has three dimensions: overall NATO strategy, and conventional and nuclear forces needed to carry out that strategy.

With respect to NATO's strategy, obviously there have been tremendous changes in the political conditions of Europe. But one basic phenomenon of European politics during these interesting times ahead will be uncertainty about the basic security environment we are likely to encounter in both the short term and the medium term, not to speak of the long term. There will be tremendous uncertainty about what the Soviet Union will be like, as well as eastern Europe. No one predicted the events of the last year, and we should not be sanguine about our ability to predict the events of the coming year.

This is not to suggest that the changes in the Soviet Union are somehow reversible. This is not to suggest that Moscow can turn back the clock and return to the era of Brezhnev. In fact, we do not believe that is possible. We believe the changes Gorbachev has made are fundamental, they are profound, and they cannot be reversed. But it is still not the same thing as being able to turn the clock ahead and see what the Soviet Union will be like three months from now, not to say three years from now.

Regardless of the changes under President Gorbachev, Soviet power will remain a major factor on the European scene. If the Soviet Union proceeds with all the reductions that it has currently pledged and the Bundeswehr goes forward with all the reductions it has planned, the Soviet armed forces three or four years from now will be many times larger than those of the Bundeswehr. Soviet forces may in fact be at least six to eight times as large as those of any other single European state, and they will be possessed by a country that dwarfs all other European states in size, population, and the number and destructive power of its nuclear weapons. Given the inevitable dominating position the Soviet Union is likely to have on the Eurasian land mass, we believe it is necessary to have American power visibly present on the continent and for that power to take a form that can respond to the tremendous uncertainty we face about the future of the European security environment. This means that in supporting its defensive strategy NATO must possess significant military power linked to both an American ground presence and to the U.S. strategic nuclear deterrent force.

In the coming years, the West will certainly face a different kind of conventional military threat than we have faced in the past when we had the threat of an overwhelming short-warning attack that offered the prospect of a theater-wide Soviet strategic offensive that might succeed. If the changes envisioned by both the Soviet leadership and by the CFE process are in fact implemented, we will face significantly different conventional defense requirements. NATO will have to adjust its conventional force structure and doctrine accordingly, and the United States is prepared to go forward with that process. NATO will be in a position to take a leading role as an agent of change in determining and coordinating the responses as shifts occur in political and military circumstances. The same holds true for our nuclear requirements.

As NATO deliberates in the next few months on what kinds of nuclear and conventional defenses we need, we should keep in mind the indispensable features that NATO must seek to preserve. Let me just mention three of these. The first is a significant U.S. military presence in Europe to demonstrate the American political and military commitment to the defense of Europe and to demonstrate the political compact of the North Atlantic Treaty through the presence of both our nuclear and conventional forces. The second is for NATO to maintain militarily significant forces in being and an evident capacity to respond to any uncertain political developments that might occur in the eastern countries whether in the nature of force regeneration or the use of current forces. And the third essential element is to keep a vital functioning international military structure poised to integrate the contributions of all allies into a meaningful common defense arrangement. If NATO maintains those essentials, it will retain the capability to respond to uncertainty without compromising its ability to deal with and adapt to change.

Another component of the new European architecture is the European Community. After a period of quiescence in the 1970s and early 1980s, the European Community has gained strength, expanded to include Spain and Portugal, and now functions as the motor of unity for western Europe both in a political and an economic sense. The United States welcomes this trend and seeks to strengthen its ties to the European Community in various ways. Early this year we announced some steps being taken in that direction, and the President and Prime Minister Haughey issued a joint communiqué announcing further initiatives. Closer cooperation with the European Community will remain an essential part of our effort to be part of Europe's future in the period ahead.

The final element of European architecture that I want to discuss in some detail is the Conference on Security and Cooperation in Europe (CSCE), the Helsinki process. I would like to agree with Mr. Shein, who commented that the importance of the CSCE had been underestimated in the United States. I think that is unquestionably true. The prestige that the CSCE has in America among certain circles is really a tribute to the work of representatives like Ambassador Kampelman in obtaining very visible improvements of human rights through the Helsinki process. But the American public has an insufficient understanding of the importance of CSCE in the European architecture of the future, and that is something we need to concentrate on improving.

The administration has a very ambitious agenda for the CSCE. But before I examine that agenda let me mention two areas where we believe the CSCE should not concentrate. First, we do not believe the CSCE is likely to play or should play an essential role in deciding the future of Germany. This task is reserved primarily for the Germans themselves. Since the four powers have special legal rights and responsibilities stemming from the Potsdam Agreement and other postwar understandings, we will have to be involved through the "two plus four" process as well. And, as dramatized by Mr. Geremek's points (Chapter 11), there will need to be reassurances to Germany's neighbors and appropriate notice taken of their interests. But the CSCE is not the forum for deciding the fate of Germany.

Similarly the administration does not believe that the CSCE is the forum for arriving at new collective security arrangements that will supersede the current alliance system. If a new structure created a commitment for every state in Europe to defend every other state under all sorts of circumstances, we would be accepting commitments that are essentially meaningless. There is a military axiom that he who tries to defend everything will defend nothing, and I think that he who promises to defend everyone will end up promising nothing. Such a security structure in which the CSCE was utilized as an umbrella for everyone to make solemn pledges to everyone else to protect them under a wide range of circumstances would amount to creating a new Kellogg-Briand Pact for Europe. This 1928 pact pledging its signatories to outlaw war was eventually signed by over sixty nations, including all the aggressor states of the 1930s, and—with the League of Nations—is generally viewed as the classic example of misplaced faith in international law and collective security. The United States will not make this mistake again in relying on the CSCE to accomplish the same sort of utopian objective. The CSCE cannot possibly accomplish this goal, because the credibility of a collective security guarantee is not provided by the treaty itself but by the actions one takes to provide evidence of intent to uphold the commitment. The collective military structure of the North Atlantic alliance and its visible unity of forces and preparedness to provide the common defense is what makes NATO a credible and effective deterrent to aggression, and it is very difficult to imagine how the CSCE could ever substitute in that role.

There is a wide range of activity in which the CSCE offers tremendous promise. The CSCE can take on new tasks in the field of security. As our French friends have pointed out, security is not limited to military issues, but it is a profoundly political concept that addresses the sources of conflict and deals with aspects of mutual insecurity as the CSCE already does in negotiating confidence- and security-building measures. But it can go beyond this and perhaps have a greater role in trying to reconcile political tensions. Some suggestions have already been made about the CSCE playing a role in crisis prevention and the management of ethnic conflicts, and these deserve further examination. The CSCE also has an enormous role to play in the economic development of Europe. The March CSCE conference in Bonn made great progress in bringing all the European states together to adopt basic principles for the transition to market principles and the development of their economies. Such an agreement on basic principles of economic development is an important contribution, and if the CSCE can move further to offer ideas and guidelines about how planned economies can make the transition to market economies, the impact can be immense. Mr. Geremek, for example, acknowledged that such a transition was a fundamental part of Poland's policy, and I think those views are shared by others in eastern Europe.

The CSCE can become an important force in the political development of Europe. I do not just speak of human rights, an area in which so much has been accomplished and where so much more can be done. But the promotion of free elections and the rule of law may also be tasks for the Helsinki process. To draw a parallel with American political development, the CSCE has already addressed itself to our Bill of Rights and now it has an opportunity to help shape other principles to guide the creation of free societies. In eastern Europe it can help illuminate the kind of political structure that guarantees stable institutions with broad pluralistic political participation overseen by the rule of law. That is an enormously ambitious goal for the CSCE, and if the CSCE can offer such guidance, it will have made a tremendous contribution to the future of Europe.

From providing political norms and institutional models, the CSCE can go even further and provide a forum for political decisionmaking. A number of leaders, most recently Prime Minister Thatcher, have put forward proposals on political development, and I would simply note that President Bush commented on Mrs. Thatcher's recent proposals in Bermuda, saying that in his view they hold great promise. We are working further to decide how the CSCE can not only provide norms for every area of political development in Europe but also provide a forum for political decisionmaking as well.

In summary, these are the elements we want to see in the evolution of Europe and America's role in it. First, we must help the countries of eastern Europe secure their revolutions and proceed with the development of democratic political and economic systems. We want to encourage the process of reform in the Soviet Union and provide norms that are applicable to all the countries in the CSCE process—East and West. Second, we want to maintain America's role as a European power. The American presence in Europe in our view is a fundamental contribution to European stability. And, third, we should strengthen and create institutions that can accommodate and coordinate military change in Europe, to enhance mutual security, guide the process of political change in Europe, and contribute to the increasing unity of Europe. If in cooperation with our European allies we can achieve these goals, we will be well on the way toward realizing the goal of a Europe whole and free.

Commentary

Discussion on security issues ranged quite broadly. A central issue was the form and mission that North Atlantic Treaty Organization (NATO) would take in coming years. Ambassador Edouard Brunner of Switzerland posed the question of how long foreign troops, especially those from the United States, would be able to stay in a united Germany. He clearly was not optimistic that they would be able to stay there in any type of organized military formations for very long. If, he argued, it proved to be the case that Germany would soon begin to call for the sharp reduction or ultimate removal of American troops, he wondered how long NATO would be able to survive without the presence of foreign troops in Germany. Ambassador Brunner also pointed out that NATO throughout its history had been a conservative force and it seemed to him very difficult for NATO to become an agent of change as President Bush and other alliance leaders have discussed in recent months.

Michael Stürmer, on the other hand, emphasized that NATO was the most important instrument for the continued stability of Europe. He thought that the continuation of a significant U.S. troop presence in Europe and in Germany was vital to maintaining the confidence of the German people in the Atlantic alliance. Many others agreed that these goals were desirable, but shared some of Ambassador Brunner's concerns about their political viability.

Closely related to the prospects for NATO was concern about the role of the United States in Europe. Rozanne Ridgway, former Assistant Secretary of State for European and Canadian Affairs, drew attention to the fact that in their papers Michael Stürmer and Georges Vaugier both emphasized a new design for Europe, a Europe larger than the present European Community and one in which the United States would have a passive and largely military role. She felt that most political leaders and specialists in the United States would insist on a more active role both in shaping and executing a new design for Europe. She argued that, if the new Europe was to be largely European designed and operated with the United States keeping a distant role of security guarantor, many Americans would come to question whether this was an appropriate role for the United States. She posed the question of whether there would really be a role for NATO and for the United States in Europe in the twenty-first century.

Closely related to Ambassador Ridgway's concerns were questions about the role of nuclear weapons in Europe. A number of participants felt there would be problems in modernizing any form of nuclear weapon to be deployed in Europe and especially in Germany and that there may well be problems in keeping nuclear weapons of any type deployed in Germany. No one was optimistic about the possibilities for modernizing short-range nuclear forces (SNF), and some pointed out that a few well-placed Germans were already expressing opposition to accepting deployment of the new tactical air-to-surface nuclear missile (TASM). Others stated that members of Congress might insist that continued American troop presence required the deployment of nuclear weapons. Some participants felt that the best solution would be to reduce the overall American force structure in Europe to about 75,000 troops who would mainly provide the basis for a reinforcement capability and guard prepositioned supplies. Such an American force posture in Europe could involve no nuclear weapons in Germany but stand-off missiles at sea and based perhaps in the United Kingdom. The major form of offensive power would be the rotation of air squadrons in and out of bases on the continent that would be kept in a modified operational capability.

A subject of great concern to everyone was how the nations of eastern Europe would provide for their security in the short and middle term. There was a great deal of discussion about a security vacuum in Central Europe and the need for the countries of eastern Europe as well as for the Soviet Union to have an organization that was able to address their security concerns. Air Vice Marshal R.A. Mason posed a more precise set of questions about the security of eastern Europe and then proceeded to answer them to the satisfaction of many in the audience. He asked what kind of security and against whom.

If the problem were internal security and issues of ethnic and nationalist strife, diplomatic pressure and the possible use of peacekeeping forces mobilized by the CSCE could handle such difficulties. If, on the other hand, the security problem were in the form of a threat from the Soviet Union, he contended that the whole structure for security would have failed and that much more fundamental change would be required. Ambassador Brunner emphasized that the CSCE was the only institution that could serve as a transitional framework for security and economic issues for the countries of eastern Europe as well as for the neutrals and nonaligned. He believed that the CSCE could be modified in a modest way to satisfy these needs until the European Community was ready to accept new members.

The appropriate role for the CSCE was also widely discussed. With the exception of the Soviet speaker, almost all of the participants shared the view of Ambassador Hans Meesman of the Netherlands that the CSCE should not be overloaded and that it could provide no adequate basis for a pan-European security organization. The clear majority opinion was that the CSCE best functioned as a process that set norms and standards of behavior and that it should not be asked to change its nature or to modify the unanimous voting requirement which proved so reassuring to the smaller countries of Europe. Several speakers with experience in the Helsinki process expressed their willingness to have one or more small secretariats established for special activities in the CSCE, and there was a general interest in exploring the possibility of the CSCE assuming limited responsibility for dealing with ethnic and border problems in eastern Europe.

The conference chairman, Max Kampelman, asked Bronisław Geremek if he saw any role for the CSCE in dealing with the question of the Polish-German border or the Lithuanian crisis. Professor Geremek said that the Polish-German border had to be a question for negotiation between the two countries and that the form of a settlement was fairly clear. Any assurances or guarantees should be made by the "two plus four" countries and could be further endorsed by a CSCE summit. Geremek emphasized that the right of self-determination should be a human right in the context of the Helsinki process and that the Helsinki II summit in 1992 should reinforce this right as well as the rights of national minorities. But with regard to Lithuania he felt it was not a question of rights but one of political realism and compromise. He expressed the hope that the Lithuanian issue could be decided through political dialogue between the Soviet and the Lithuanian leaderships.

Ambassador Brunner expressed the view of many that the CSCE should not be turned into an institution, nor should it be used to negotiate a peace treaty concluding World War II. He was willing to explore a role for the CSCE in ethnic and border conflicts and even thought that it might be possible for Switzerland to participate in such activities. Brunner proposed taking the Open Skies negotiations out of the talks on conventional forces in Europe (CFE) and putting them into the CSCE process so that all confidence- and security-building measures (CSBMs) would be together.

The discussion on the security section concluded with a statement by George Vest, former Director-General of the U.S. Foreign Service, that the world is extremely fortunate to have three institutions so vital and strong as the CSCE, NATO, and the European Community.

III. Economic Integration and Restructuring

Chapter 13

Lessons from the Marshall Plan

Alan Milward

It seems to have become a convention of recent discussion to equate the U.S. aid program to western Europe after 1948 with what might now be needed as a recovery program for eastern Europe. How realistic a comparison is it and what can be learned from it?

The most commonly encountered suggestions for a recovery program for eastern Europe run along the following lines. Although its purpose would be general, it would also have to have country-specific objectives. An aid program for Poland with its $40 billion in foreign debt, its free prices, its high labor mobility, its 850,000 officially unemployed, its liberalized banking system, and its free access to world markets could scarcely have identical objectives to one for Bulgaria, with a debt of about $10 billion, a centrally planned economy, no labor mobility, no officially recognized unemployment, and a strictly controlled foreign trade sector. Second, it would have to have an initial emergency component of aid-in-kind, notably to Romania but also perhaps to Poland. Third, it would have to tackle the whole question of debt relief. This could not be tackled without specific commitments to stabilization and to reform of the banking and fiscal systems where they remain unchanged. Czechoslovakia, the German Democratic Republic (GDR), and Romania still have banking systems in which there is no effective separation between central and commercial banking. Only Hungary, Poland, and Yugoslavia have attempted anti-inflationary stabilization programs by a combination of fiscal and monetary policy and the latter two have the highest inflation rates in Europe. Even the Hungarian inflation rate is close to 20 percent annually. In all the others suppressed inflation constrains future economic policy choices. Fourth, the inadequate bilateral trading machinery between these economies would have to be replaced by some more satisfactory multilateral trading mechanism. This would mean some machinery for currency transferability at relatively stable and non-artificial exchange rates, or even, as many in those countries argue, full currency convertibility. Last, debts are only likely to be paid off by a better balance of commodity trade and this means manufactured exports of a higher and more widely acceptable quality. That in turn seems to mean project-specific credits for industrial restructuring.

Some of the elements of a program of this kind are already present in the PHARE (Pologne Hongrie Assistance à la Reconstruction Economique) of the Commission of the European Communities. The program includes emergency food supplies, guaranteed export credits, direct loans, and a special ECU (European Currency Unit) fund in the European Investment Bank, raised worldwide but guaranteed by the Community, for joint ventures and for national infrastructural investment in both countries. The initial procedures of this program did in fact somewhat resemble the Marshall Plan, because the Polish government was required to draw up a specific list of import requirements. And, the cynic might add, it was no more coherent than the "shopping-lists" drawn up by the West European countries in 1948. This program although it was extended in February falls far short in scope of the range of objectives set out in the previous paragraph and it is limited to two countries. It is this which suggests to so many commentators that something more of the scope of the Marshall Plan is required.

The analogy with the Marshall Plan has usually been presented in an extremely optimistic light, as though injecting into the piecemeal aid programs for eastern Europe comprehensive global objectives like those of the Marshall Plan and a demand for a prior commitment to these objectives from all the aid recipients would by itself guarantee that most of the objectives which such a program could aim at would be achieved. To this is sometimes added the even more optimistic gloss that a Marshall Plan for eastern Europe would serve as a

Keynesian project in the West and help to increase levels of employment. How far did the objectives of the Marshall Plan coincide with the scope of the recovery program for eastern Europe as it is presently discussed?

It was never a primary purpose of the Marshall Plan to provide emergency aid or aid-in-kind, even though that was effectively what it did do for the western zones of Austria and Germany in its first year. Food was 48.6 percent of all European Recovery Program shipments to Germany in the first year of the program (1949) and 77.7 percent of those to Austria. In this sense it has to be seen as supplemental there to the military relief programs (Government Aid and Relief in Occupied Areas). Although official rations in Germany (if they were obtainable) and the average unrationed level of calorific intake in Italy in the first year of the European Recovery Program were actually lower than the present Romanian ration (if it is available) and lower too than the availability of food to those Poles reduced to genuine hardship by monetary and fiscal reform, where aid funds were used for food imports this was more commonly a decision by American military authorities than by aid receiving governments. European governments had other priorities.

The purpose for which aid was sought and used was to finance imports of capital goods, steel, and transport equipment. It is this which was the main characteristic of the Marshall Plan. In retrospect its first achievement was to succeed in financing the continuation of high levels of capital goods imports into European economies, already very high because of the extremely high capital investment ratios which had prevailed since the end of the war, but threatened from summer 1947 onward by the shortage of dollars in international trade. In a world where German supply had been almost eliminated, the United States had become the only possible supplier of capital goods on the scale needed. At first therefore aid financed imports of investment goods from the United States. As Germany recovered it then was used to finance investment goods imports from the Federal Republic. As soon as we ask what the level of capital goods imports into eastern Europe would have to be to achieve similar increases in industrial output and exports the inappropriateness of the comparison becomes apparent.

Three countries, Portugal, which received very little aid, and Greece and Turkey, which also received special direct aid from the United States outside the Marshall Plan, were the only participants in the European Recovery Program which were not highly developed economies, either with an already existing sophisticated industrial sector supplying a wide range of goods for export or with the capacity, like the Netherlands or Denmark, very quickly to develop one. The rapid and sustained increases in the value and volume of inter-West European trade from 1948 to 1958 can be listed as the second achievement of the Marshall Plan and they certainly have lessons to offer to eastern Europe in the way in which they were achieved. But it is important to bear in mind that they would not have been achieved without the existence of Germany. It was not only that Germany was already in the 1930s an exporter of capital goods on the same scale as the United States that made the Marshall Plan work, nor was it the level of economic development of the aid recipients. It was, perhaps even more important, the German market. Trade to the Federal Republic in those sectors of finished manufactured goods which had the highest component of research and development expenditure and the highest proportions of value added grew faster from virtually every West European country than did German exports of the same products to them, although of course the gap in absolute levels was still very wide. Germany became within two years of the Marshall Plan the pivot of western Europe's trade and payments system, and although the resolute pursuit of a multilateral payments framework by the Marshall planners had much to do with that, the specific historical circumstances of the Federal Republic had even more to do with it. With no reserves, with low levels of wages and low levels of personal disposable income, and with the population increasing at an alarming rate, there was no conceivable alternative choice of economic policy in the Federal Republic than to concentrate on exports. It is this which accounts for the much lower levels of protectionism there than in the other major West European economies in the 1950s and for the rapid emergence of a commercial symbiosis between the Federal Republic and the many developed small trade-dependent West European economies for which protectionism and bilateral trade offered no reasonable future.

Today's Realities

Could western Europe and/or the United States now play a similar role for eastern Europe? The answer must be a pessimistic one, first because eastern Europe with the possible exception of Hungary does not have much that western economies would want to buy in suitable quantities, and second because with different political consensus commercial policies in the West have changed.

It is this which makes it crucially important not to offer to eastern Europe a myth about the links between the Marshall Plan, foreign trade, and currency stabilization. The 1950s were in fact a relatively protectionist decade and also one in which the Rooseveltian ambitions for global multilateralism based on currency convertibility had no place. To preach anything approaching free trade and instant currency convertibility to eastern Europe is to travesty the Marshall Plan and, if the lessons of history count, to court disaster.

The currently prevailing idea that stabilization of East European economies must necessarily include widespread privatization, the introduction of equilibrating money and stock markets, and an almost complete dissolution of existing planning and controls is an understandable reaction to the lamentable economic performance of centrally controlled East European economies over the last twenty years. The mood in 1947 was quite different. As historians have shown, the prevailing ideology then was a mixture of American New Deal and European postwar "Keynesian" capitalism. The Economic Cooperation Administration was a great deal more critical of the restrictive monetary policies of Italian central bankers than it was of the economic controls imposed by French or Norwegian planners with whose objectives it was in close sympathy. In the interwar period it was free-market capitalist economies which had not performed well. The politico-economic objective of the Marshall Plan was to stabilize western Europe by fostering the evolution of a modern, modified capitalism in which the influence of central government over allocatory decisions would play a larger role. The harmony of political agreement on this issue between postwar governing elites in western Europe and the United States was also, it should be added, much closer than the current spread of political opinion about social and economic objectives between West and East. Closer, too, it seems than the spread within the West itself.

Suppressed inflation was usually kept in check, not too successfully, by a battery of economic controls which in many countries lasted well into the 1950s. Only in the western zones of Germany, where controls broke down under the impact of occupation and the administrative disruption caused by the divided and improvised military administrations, was there a drastic monetary reform, with a rapidly widening spread of incomes, as in Poland over the last year. The much-cited Belgian monetary reform was more a matter of rhetoric and gesture than practice and an equally common attitude was that of French planners who took the view that the best case for suppressed inflation was more goods, even if this meant very large deficits on commodity account.

The liberalization of trade and payments in western Europe which the Marshall Plan initiated was a much more gradual process than anything the Polish or Hungarian governments are being encouraged to attempt. The Organization for European Economic Cooperation trade liberalization program removed quotas only on trade as measured by its 1948 volumes. It excluded all imports on government account in a period when many governments still imported a large proportion of agricultural imports through state trading agencies. From November 1951 the United Kingdom and from February 1952 France, the two largest importers, deserted the scheme for a long period. Even by 1956 quotas had still not been removed even on the 1948 trade levels, although the intervening period had witnessed one of the most remarkable periods of growth in intra–West European trade on record. Tariff reductions were even less noticeable. After the initial efforts made in Torquay and Annecy, the General Agreement on Tariffs and Trade after 1949 was merely a vehicle for sustaining protectionism. Commercial policy was a well-calculated mixture of a gradually liberalizing trend and trade restrictions supporting national industrial restructuring policies through specific links between industrial and commercial policies. The case of the quotas and subsidies used to protect and develop the Italian car and steel industries in an otherwise increasingly open economy would be a perfect example, and one which can easily be reproduced in every West European country. Very little

Marshall Aid went on specific industrial restructuring projects. They were achieved because the only restrictions placed on them by the trade and payments machinery were the cooperation and mutual concessions in commercial policy which the OEEC framework imposed.

As for the payments mechanism it advanced toward a limited convertibility with equal caution, especially so in comparison with the bold aspirations for speedy worldwide convertibility expressed in the Bretton Woods agreements and sometimes voiced now by East European politicians. Transferability was guaranteed by the European Payments Union after 1950. Convertibility for citizens in unrestricted amounts as a legal right remained, though, largely a myth in the western world, used for demonstrating logical points in economics text books but not having much to do with the real operations of multilateral trade since the Marshall Plan. Only the Swiss franc, the Belgian franc, and the Deutschmark have been effectively fully and freely convertible for most of that time. The Deutschmark has been so only since 1959. Even after January 1959 when more West European currencies became legally convertible into dollars a range of exchange controls remained on the statute books and it was not until the early 1960s that convertibility into dollars was followed by the removal of trade discrimination against dollar imports.

In so far as it is valid to draw lessons from the Marshall Plan the lessons would therefore seem to be the following. A successful and a peaceful reform of the domestic economic policies and political structures of East European countries is a vital interest of western Europe and the United States, but it could be achieved by a coordinated recovery program only if there was close agreement between elites in West and East. Agreement depends on the emerging nature of new political consensuses on each side. They remain most unclear compared to the picture in 1947. A transitional period, probably a lengthy one, of controls on trade and currency relations is indispensable for successful adjustment. Credits for re-equipment would be best linked to foreign trade and to a commitment to the pursuit of multilateral trade. But there should be, as there was under the Marshall Plan, a large mutual element of aid included in the clearing mechanisms. West European countries were able to buy German exports in the quantities they did before 1956 only because the generous credits allowed to debtors in the European Payments Union clearing mechanism effectively forced the Federal Republic to find its own exports, when it might otherwise have demanded gold or local currency for them. This would mean dismantling the Council for Mutual Economic Assistance trade and payments framework. Convertible currencies will not be securely established without a lengthy period of exchange controls. None of this could be achieved without a regular consultative framework in which the extent of mutual concessions can be determined. In that framework Germany and the Soviet Union would have to be the two most important members. And last it would have to be accepted that this would not constitute a Keynesian recovery program for the West, except for the two countries whose exports would be the principal beneficiaries, Germany and Italy.

Chapter 14

West European Economic Integration and East European Disintegration

Josef C. Brada

At the same time that many West European countries are moving confidently toward 1992, the economies of eastern Europe are moving, with much less confidence and certainty but with at least as much hope, toward a new economic future. While the specific means of achieving this new future remain unclear, the broad outlines of their goals and means of reaching them may be discerned. The East European countries seek to achieve more productive and prosperous economies by means of a greater reliance on markets and private property. These developments in the two parts of Europe interact with each other in various ways. In the realm of economics, it is clear that the trade of eastern Europe will be reoriented toward the West and that the flows of capital, technology, and business know-how between the two parts of Europe will increase.

While in general such an increase in trade and investment between the halves of Europe should have positive effects, the ability of governments to influence the distribution of these benefits among countries and to manage the social and political consequences of these expanded economic contacts need to be examined. Currently East-West relations are evolving in a variety of ways: through bilateral country-to-country contacts, through relations between individual countries and international organizations such as the General Agreement on Tariffs and Trade, through relations between individual countries and supernational organizations such as the European Community (EC), and within regional integration blocs such as the Community, the European Free Trade Association (EFTA), and the Council for Mutual Economic Assistance (Comecon). However, most of these organizations were formed at a different time and for different purposes. In general these organizations were set up to achieve the objectives of groups of like-minded countries with similar economic systems. Whether organizations constituted in this way will be reasonably able to deal with the problems of countries transitioning from state planning and social ownership to a more market-oriented system is at this point unclear. The fact that most of these organizations were formed in ways that did not span across the two halves of Europe suggests that their ability to serve as a bridge between East and West in this period of rapid economic, political, and social change needs to be examined with some care, and if present organizations are found to be lacking, then thought must be given to forming new ones.

The Economic Landscape in Eastern Europe

At this time, the countries of eastern Europe differ in their conceptions of the objectives of economic reforms and in the pace at which they wish to implement these reforms. Some, such as Czechoslovakia, Hungary, and Poland appear to be aiming at the creation of systems where markets and the role of private property predominate. Other countries, such as the USSR, Bulgaria, and Romania have not entirely abandoned directive planning as the principal means of allocating resources and the role of private production continues to be seen as an auxiliary rather than dominant form of business organization. Nevertheless, starting as they are from economic systems where state-ownership is virtually all-encompassing in industry, where market forces have been subjugated by directive plans, where relative prices are far from equilibrium, and where many of the institutions that are necessary for the functioning of a capitalist market economy are only now being constructed, it is important to conceive of how they will be organized and how they will function.

Privatization will proceed slowly whatever the intention of policymakers. This is principally due to the fact that in none of these countries is there a desire simply to hand over ownership to the population by means of some sort of social distribution of property rights. Thus state-owned enterprises will be sold to domestic residents, to workers through various employee stock-ownership plan (ESOP) schemes, and to foreign investors. However, domestic savings are a fraction of the book value of industrial capital, and there does not exist a domestic financial system capable of financing the purchase of state-owned assets. Moreover, policymakers seem disinclined to sell state property at prices that would reflect the level of liquid savings in these countries.

This imbalance between the capital stock and liquid savings suggests that in both the more reformist as well as in the less reform-minded economies, there will continue to be a large state-owned sector in industry, managed by some combination of state-appointed managers, workers' councils, and managers who will lease and operate state-owned property. The state sector will coexist and compete with private firms that have been purchased by foreign firms, by domestic financial institutions, and by home-country residents. In addition, there will be privatization from below, as the formation of, mainly small, private businesses is allowed. These natural barriers to a rapid privatization of the capital stock will be augmented by widely shared perceptions that communications, transportation, public utilities, and other public services should remain in state hands.

The distorted nature of relative prices, as well as monetary disequilibria, have made reformers cautious about price reform. Too rapid a freeing of prices is seen as being fraught with danger. In part this is because reformers are pessimistic about the downward flexibility of prices, believing that even relative price changes would have an inflationary impact, while the existence of pent-up purchasing power is seen as a barrier to price flexibility in all countries save Poland. Moreover, to the extent that prices are flexible downward, a too rapid realignment carries with it the danger of unacceptable levels of unemployment. Thus both the desire to limit the pace and range of relative price changes and the distortion by inflationary forces of the information conveyed by prices suggests that markets will not, over the course of the transition, provide the quantity or type of information available in developed market economies.

Probably the least effective but most important markets will be those for capital. While most reforms call for converting state enterprises into joint-stock companies, this in itself will not guarantee the creation of efficient equity or credit markets. The newly formed joint stock companies will be closely held, either by the government, by a small group of commercial banks, by specially organized holding companies, by worker ESOPs, or by foreigners. Each of these owners will tend to hold large blocs of shares and will have little interest, or, in the case of ESOPs, ability to trade shares actively on the market. Thus the obstacles to valuing the shares of these firms through an efficient equities market will be similar to those encountered in the valuation of the stock of closely held firms in market economies.

On the credit side, Hungary and Czechoslovakia have created a network of commercial banks in the hope that these would impose financial discipline on firms seeking loans. Unfortunately, these commercial banks were saddled with the outstanding loans of existing state enterprises. Many of these loans were issued at the behest of planners on the basis of criteria other than profitability at either past or prospective prices, and consequently many of them are likely to cause problems for enterprises and banks alike. Thus both the supply of bank credit, and the terms under which it is available may not fully reflect market conditions.

At the same time, the pressure on capital markets will be intense. The volume of investment will probably fall as consumers will be able to compete for goods more effectively than they could in the past when the enterprise sector operated on a soft budget constraint. At the same time, important capital allocation decisions will have to be made. In part there will be a need for difficult capital allocation decisions due to the need to restructure and reduce the bloated industrial structures of these countries. Which firms or, given the size of firms in these countries, which sectors of industry are to be eliminated and which are to survive will have to be decided relatively quickly. Foreign trade will be reallocated toward the West, and thus at the same time that some sectors of industry are being eliminated others will require new infusions of capital and technology in order to compete in western markets. Emerging private firms are likely to be undercapitalized and thus will have a strong demand for credit, particularly if this sector experiences a rapid growth in demand. Lending to these firms, however, will be risky, both because of their fragile financial foundations and because of the inexperience of their owners.

In sum, in even the most reform-minded of the economies of eastern Europe, the role of the state as an allocator of resources, and especially of investment resources, as well as owner of industrial enterprises will remain an important if not dominant feature of the economic mechanism. At the same time market-generated signals will be weak, will contain much noise, and will also be subject to considerable misinterpretation by economic agents unaccustomed to functioning in a market environment. In economies where less radical reforms are envisioned, the weakness of market signals, of course, will be even greater and the role of the state correspondingly stronger.

Implications for Eastern Europe

The expansion of East-West economic relations during the process of reform is often viewed as largely the responsibility of the East European countries. This is in part because the systems they are now abandoning are seen as the principal barriers to these relations. The autarkic tendencies of planners, the nontransparency of the foreign trade mechanism, the inconvertibility and overvaluation of national currencies, irrational price system, and the inward-looking development strategies of Comecon are all seen as self-inflicted limitations on the ability of East European countries to participate in international economic relations more fully. If these countries would only eliminate these barriers and adopt the principles of the GATT and the Bretton Woods institutions, the popular view holds, then the benefits of freer trade would quickly follow. In reality, especially in the short run, there are likely to be some serious negative consequences for eastern Europe from expanded East-West economic relations, and it behooves us to ask whether existing economic institutions and the principles they espouse will be capable of dealing with the political and social as well as economic costs of the transition period.

The reorientation of eastern Europe's trade toward the West will have to be slow, in part because of the magnitude of East European–Soviet trade and the difficulty of adjusting both East European products and world markets to such a realignment. With a good deal of East European industry remaining in state hands and relative prices continuing to be somewhat distorted, the possibilities for free trade, or at least a significantly less administratively controlled trade are circumscribed. The pent-up purchasing power of East European consumers and the technological backwardness of East European industry coupled with the need to update and restructure productive capacity will represent a tremendous demand for western goods. This, as well as trade decisions that appear rational on the basis of existing, but distorted, prices will be forces with which these economies will have to deal. At the same time the attempt to generate greater exports to the West may be met by protectionist measures, either explicit or implicit.

Existing western organizations are not well-equipped to deal with such issues. The GATT, for example, has a poor record of dealing with nonmarket economies characterized by extensive state involvement in trade decisions. At the same time, the pace at which East European countries can convert themselves into market economies will be slow. Thus the question will arise, at what level of privatization or what level of marketization do these countries qualify for GATT membership. Indeed, it is not at all obvious that their economic interests will be served by attempting to accede to GATT practices as rapidly as possible. Free trade will bring with it social conflict between workers and owners in sectors that expand or contract as a result of expanded East-West trade, and such structural changes may have important regional consequences, causing interregional or interethnic strife.

A second instrument for promoting East-West trade has been the series of bilateral agreements negotiated between the European Community and individual East European countries. While the reduction of barriers to East European exports to the Community is to be welcomed, the use of the European Community as an instrument to achieve these ends, even if desired by the Soviet Union and eastern Europe, raises serious problems. One is that it excludes those western countries who are not members of the European Community to compete for the same sort of "special relationship." Thus what may emerge from EC–East European contacts is a strengthening of an undesirable tendency to create such special relationships between trading blocs. Thus the European Community's efforts vis-à-vis eastern Europe can be interpreted in the same fashion as its initiatives toward the developing countries with whom they have sought out a special relationship. One may then wonder whether EC diplomacy is more geared toward expanding East-West trade in general or more in making eastern Europe a preserve for EC interests much in the way that the East German economy is viewed as something to be swallowed up by, and incorporated into, the West German one.

What eastern Europe does not need is "special relations" that further distort trade decisions in an environment already replete with distortions. The trade policy issues before eastern Europe are relatively straightforward. First there is that part of East European production that consists of low-value-to-weight industrial inputs such as steel, cement, metal products, basic chemicals, etc. A fundamental problem is to integrate this production into the West European industrial supply system. Thus Polish steel needs to be able to make its way, on a regular basis, to Mercedes factories in West Germany, to be combined there with Czechoslovak glass and Hungarian leather to make West German cars. Given the nature of the East European exports, they cannot travel far in this form, and thus their utilization in western Europe is largely a European problem, and a serious one. For eastern Europe, it will determine how much of its industrial plant will survive. For western Europe serious problems will also arise, partly because western Europe has just completed a painful and costly structural readjustment in the very smokestack industries that will now face this new East European competition. Eastern Europe will have to do more than export semifabricates and materials. Finished products for consumers and firms, with a higher share of value added to materials, will also have to be directed toward western markets. An examination of the markets for these types of goods quickly reveals that economies of scale often dictate global markets. Eastern Europe must have the will and the way to market these goods not only in the European Community, but also in North America and the Far East. Agreements with the European Community will do little to help foster this latter sort of trade. The involvement of American and Japanese firms, and the existence of the underlying commercial framework for facilitating these trade flows will be critical.

This need for a systematic effort to develop the ways and means of integrating eastern Europe into international trade is pressing. Suggestions that it can be done simply by advising East European governments to opt for markets and free trade ignore the critical and difficult transition that these countries face. At the same time neither the GATT nor the Bretton Woods institutions appears capable of evolving new mechanisms or ways of dealing with the problems of expanded East-West trade. What is needed is a broader-based approach to the integration of eastern Europe into the global economy, one that goes beyond the parochial interests of the European Community, although of course, many of the European Community's objectives must play a key role in this global program. A new institution is needed, and participants in this organization could develop mutually acceptable mechanisms for the reduction of East-West trade barriers and technology export restrictions, for the financing of East-West trade, for dealing with dumping charges, and for mitigating the costs of structural readjustment in the East and in the West. While the European Community would necessarily play a key role in such an organization, other countries must also be able to make a contribution.

The opening of eastern Europe to capital flows from the West will also create difficulties. The existing lack of information about the value of firms or of their profitability results both from poor accounting procedures and from distorted domestic prices. Thus there are ample opportunities for exploitative investment behavior on the part of western buyers or for missed opportunities by East European sellers. In Hungary, there has already been a series of scandals in connection with the sale or attempted sale of Hungarian enterprises to foreigners at prices that failed to reflect either any realistic assessment of these firms' earning ability or the value of their assets. At the same time, fears of being "taken" on the part of the Polish government must have played a part in the breakdown of negotiations with Barbara Piasecka-Johnson for the sale of the Lenin Shipyard in Gdansk.

Nevertheless, foreign investors are likely to play a large role in privatization efforts in those countries that allow them sufficient scope for their efforts. Only foreign investors are able to raise the credits needed to buy up the overlarge industrial plants that have been built up in eastern Europe. Moreover, only foreign investors will have the technology, business know-how, and connections to world markets to integrate the output of the East European economies to international markets in the way discussed above.

While the role of foreign investors in privatization and restructuring is important, there are also risks and dangers. Foreign ownership of the means of production is always a touchy political issue, even in economies whose populations accept the need to be responsive to the workings of the world market and recognize the benefits of expanded trade and investment, and where prosperity and stable economic conditions reign. In countries where workers are used to being insulated from the shocks of the world economy, where paternalism and full employment have been the key economic benefits of the system, efforts by foreign owners to respond flexibly to evolving market conditions may face political resistance. This resistance will likely be intensified because many East European governments are looking to foreign investors to take the measures to reduce costs and overstaffing and to liquidate unprofitable operations that the governments themselves deem too unpopular to undertake on their own.

Foreign investment will also have important regional and environmental consequences. West European governments may seek to induce their firms to locate facilities that are more pollution-intensive in eastern Europe in order to alleviate their own environmental problems. Since the industries of eastern Europe are biased toward "dirty" sectors, such efforts need not require large infusions of new capital, and modest improvements may make East European plants competitive with those operating in western Europe under more stringent environmental restrictions. But concerned citizens in eastern Europe may object on environmental grounds to this emphasis on pollution-intensive industry. Another source of investor-host society conflict may arise over regional development efforts of the government. These are often in conflict with the objectives of foreign investors, who seek the benefits of good infrastructure often found in more developed regions. What, for example, will be the political consequences of large western investments into Czech industry near Prague and the Federal Republic of Germany, and low investments in more distant and less accessible Slovakia? Or of German investments in Transylvania at the expense of Bucharest?

The creation of the Bank for European Reconstruction and Development is a useful step, but it does not address many of the problems raised here. Western investors should be encouraged to seek out legitimate investment opportunities in eastern Europe. At the same time East European governments and populations should not have to feel that simply in order to join the world economy they have to put their entire economies up for sale at a chaotic and frequently irrational rummage sale. Means should be developed to empower residents of these countries to obtain ownership of productive assets within their own countries, not only as a matter of social justice but also for the practical political necessity of retaining support for further economic reform. An international conference should be set up to develop a code of conduct for investors in eastern Europe and to consider means whereby East European residents could gradually reacquire ownership in their factories and farms. Large infusions of capital are not needed by eastern Europe. In the short run, such infusions are likely to be misused, in part because of distorted prices and in part because the ability of these economies to absorb capital may well be below the current level of domestic saving. Throwing money at East European problems may worsen rather than help the situation.

Centrifugal Forces and Eastern Europe

Eastern Europe is subject to a variety of strong centrifugal forces whose effects may be less beneficial than initially anticipated. On the economic front, the strengthening of European Community integration is clearly pulling each individual East European country toward the European Community, encouraging them to sign trade agreements, consider associate status, and look forward to eventual membership. The European Community's bargaining strategy of bypassing the Comecon and dealing only with individual countries clearly strengthened the centrifugal forces acting on eastern Europe. At the same time, the centripetal force of Comecon integration has sharply diminished. The Soviet Union has adopted a policy of benign neglect toward the organization, and spokesmen for the reforming countries are claimed to have argued for dollars and markets to replace Comecon integration. Moreover, different reform conceptions and foreign trade strategies among

Comecon's members reduce the organization's ability to promote trade among its members.

There are, of course, elements of Comecon integration that need to be discarded, the various schemes for investment specialization and scientific technical progress chief among them. Such policies were both ineffective and inward-looking and are irrelevant to economies seeking to integrate themselves into the world economy.

At the same time, many of the trade flows among the Comecon countries make good economic sense, reflect comparative advantages, and ought not be disrupted. It need not be the case that all Soviet imports of Hungarian televisions be replaced by Panasonics, or that all Soviet oil exports to Czechoslovakia be replaced by imports from Saudi Arabia. Many firms in Comecon countries have long-standing relationships with clients in other Comecon members, and often these reflect considerable adjustment and response to individual needs. The Comecon trade mechanism, which facilitates government-to-government trade decisions may indeed prove to be a valuable way of maintaining economically justified trade among the Comecon countries. Western undermining of Comecon integration, by differentiating among Comecon members on the basis of their politics, by trying to wean East European countries from the Comecon, and by encouraging these countries to abandon their regional trade preferences in favor of free trade may well be eliminating a valuable source of economic strength from eastern Europe's ability to help itself. These centrifugal forces are, of course, exacerbated by political factors, as regional and ethnic tensions have risen both within and among Comecon members.

Comecon can play a valuable role by continuing to facilitate trade and investment flows among members. The visits of East European delegations to Moscow this spring to discuss such possibilities are a positive sign. No doubt changes in both the means and the objectives of Comecon integration are needed, but some form of integration among these countries can play a positive role in their reconstruction.

Conclusion

The emerging economies and societies of eastern Europe are fragile but are being subjected to strong pressures by western models of behavior and to the structures dictated by western institutions. While such demands may accurately reflect the long-term evolution of the East European countries, in the transition period they impose heavy costs on the reforming economies. Perhaps new and more supportive international organizations are needed to see eastern Europe through its transition.

Commentary

In commenting on the two papers presented in this section, Jan Vanous, President and Research Director of PlanEcon, Inc. of Washington, D.C., said that he found no really useful lessons could be derived from the Marshall Plan. He expressed clear opposition to any type of food aid to eastern Europe, because it would hurt the farmers of that region. He emphasized the need for the creation of market infrastructure such as stock and bond markets, mechanisms for commercial banking, communications, accounting, and insurance. There is, he said, an immense need for economic and business education of a very practical and western sort. Vanous pointed out the need among all East European economies for transition financial assistance. Without it the Soviet conversion to hard currency trade at the end of 1990 could cause a drop in East European prices of up to 60 percent, thus creating a severe recession. This type of incident coupled with the multiplier effect of six or seven countries converting to more open trade at the same time could lead to disaster for the region.

Hans Decker, President of the Siemens Corporation in New York, spoke from a practical business perspective on the needs of Central Europe. He pointed out that his corporation, Siemens, had in recent years derived roughly 1 percent of its total revenues from business activities in eastern Europe and the Soviet Union combined. He believes that eastern Europe needs a combination of a large number of small private ventures and the creation of infrastructure of the sort that Jan Vanous recommended. Drawing on the experience of the Siemens Corporation, he pointed out that contacts with East Europeans could be extremely helpful in making joint ventures work. He gave examples of how businessmen and officials from the German Democratic Republic had already proved very useful in helping corporations of the Federal Republic gain access to East European markets, transportation, and credit.

John Evans, Coordinator of CSCE Affairs at the U.S. Department of State, provided a brief report on the results of the Bonn CSCE conference on economic affairs in March. This conference did endorse a U.S.-originated statement of the desirability of open markets and their key role in supporting political democracy, and he pointed out that the strongest support for this U.S. position came from the East Europeans themselves. The West Europeans, he felt, had been much less enthusiastic about this proposal because of the somewhat ideological tone of the document and a desire not to offend the Soviet Union.

The most powerful statement in the discussion came from Michael Stürmer who expanded upon the arguments of the two papers at this session to draw bleak conclusions for the prospects of stability in eastern Europe. He expressed confidence that in five years the German Democratic Republic will be fully integrated into the Federal Republic of Germany, declaring: "In ten years Dresden will be another Munich." But he contended that the rest of eastern Europe was another case altogether. The research at his institute and other findings that he has seen indicate that Poland is not at all well organized for economic reform and will have a difficult time; Hungary because of its entrepreneurial tradition will do fairly well; and Czechoslovakia is somewhere in between these two. All the rest of the East European economies will have great difficulty moving toward open markets. For the region as a whole he fears widespread unemployment and social and ethnic strife. Since the western countries have linked democracy with prosperity, such economic and social difficulties could produce a major reaction against democracy and the rise of strong authoritarian nationalist movements, perhaps leading to new authoritarian governments. This in a fairly short number of months could become a major problem with economic, political, and security dimensions.

IV. Human and Political Rights

Chapter 15

Fundamental Rights and the Hungarian Constitution of 1989

Péter Paczolay

The radical political transformations in eastern Europe have created a basically new situation regarding the enforcement and protection of human rights. Formerly only a small democratic opposition has opposed dictatorship and in its fight has appealed to human rights. After the collapse of the Communist party's dictatorship, the newly established pluralist parliamentary democracy will positively safeguard human rights. In the new constitutional order a democratic Hungary, contrary to the former empty declarations, will actually fulfil the obligations accepted in international agreements.

Fundamental Rights in the Hungarian Constitution

The first written constitution in the history of Hungary was promulgated by Act XX of 1949. This constitution was strongly influenced by the Soviet constitution of 1936 (known also as the Stalin constitution). It has undergone several amendments, for example, in 1972 the thesis on the leading role of the Marxist-Leninist party was introduced in its text. As a consequence of the fundamental political changes beginning in 1988, it became necessary to create a basically new constitution. The Communist party and the opposition agreed to make major amendments to the 1949 constitution and to leave the drafting of a new constitution to the new parliament that was freely elected in March 1990.

The amended constitution was promulgated on October 23, 1989, "with a view to promote a peaceful political transition to a constitutional State implementing a multi-party system, parliamentary democracy, and a social market economy"—as the preamble declares. The amended constitution states that Hungary is a republic and an independent, democratic, constitutional state. Political parties may be freely formed and operate freely, but none of the parties or other organizations of citizens shall direct their activities toward acquiring, violently exercising, or exclusively wielding power.

The original constitution of 1949—just as its model, the Stalin constitution of 1936—did not recognize abstract human rights, but the state "assured" civil rights and freedoms corresponding to "the interest of the people." According to the 1972 modification, this phrase was changed to read "to the interest of socialism and the people." The regulation of civil rights in the socialist constitutions is characterized by the ambivalence that citizens' rights are listed comprehensively and guaranteed formally, but in reality they do not matter and are frequently curtailed by legislation.

As for Hungary, the modified 1989 constitution has changed these shortcomings. Chapter XII of the constitution, entitled Fundamental Rights and Duties, has been revised, and the general provisions in Chapter I also include some basic rights. Article 8, paragraph 1 of the constitution declares: "The Republic of Hungary recognizes the inviolable and inalienable fundamental human rights." The general provisions guarantee among others the right of inheritance, recognize the right to a healthy environment, and mention such institutions related to basic rights as property, marriage, family, and social policy.

The rights and freedoms provided by Chapter XII include the right to life and human dignity, to liberty and personal safety, to be judged in a just and public hearing by an independent and unprejudiced court, to defense in criminal procedures, to claim for remedy, to move and select one's residence, to reputation, to inviolability of domicile, to protection of private secrets, to freedom of thought, conscience, and religion; freedom of speech; liberty of press, of assembly, and of association, of complaint to a state organ, of asylum for persecuted persons; right to education; rights of national and lingual minorities; right to vote and to be voted, to work, to physical and mental health, to social security; freedom of scientific and artistic life; and equal rights in every aspect. This shows that the modified constitution recognizes a great number of fundamental rights as well as political and social rights. This new statement of human rights has tried to conform to the international declarations in this field, such as the Universal Declaration of Human Rights, the 1966 International Covenant on Human Rights (to which Hungary has acceded), and the European Convention on Human Rights (which Hungary intends to accept).

Among the main characteristics of the new statement of basic rights, a fundamental conceptual change has to be emphasized. While the former text of the constitution acknowledged only the category of "citizens' rights," the new one reflects the idea of inviolable and inalienable "human rights," and these human rights are not bound to citizenship but are due to all human beings. The reference to "inalienable" rights undoubtedly demonstrates the revival of a natural law principle denied for forty years. Socialist ideology has rejected classifications like "innate" and "inalienable" rights. Now Hungarian legal philosophers emphasize the essential universality of human and civil rights, viewing them as the fundamental and lasting values of mankind.

The Hierarchy of Constitutional Provisions

The fundamental law of the Hungarian legal system is the constitution of 1949. Previously the basic conditions of the constitutional order were regulated in a series of fundamental laws originating at different historical times from the thirteenth century forward. In 1949 a new, "socialist" constitution was promulgated that embraced all the constitutional provisions. All acts and other legal instruments had to be in conformity with the constitution, reflecting the principle of supremacy of the constitution over all other laws and decrees. The special position of the constitution in the hierarchy of law was strengthened by the provision that a two-thirds majority vote of the members of parliament was required for enacting or amending the constitution.

Moreover, the whole hierarchy of laws is based on the *lex superior* principle: a law of lower rank shall not conflict with legal sources of higher rank. The *lex superior* principle is not included in the constitution, but is stated in Article 1, paragraph 2 of Act XI of 1987 regulating the order of legislation.

The 1949 constitution was a "closed" system of rules, including all the constitutional requirements. It was characterized by a high generality and abstraction of its provisions. Due to the declarative and programmatic nature of that constitution, the courts could not accept constitutional provisions as direct grounds for their decisions. Consequently, a series of ordinary statutes served as "executory" laws, giving the abstract constitutional provisions a concrete, positive form.

In the amended 1989 constitution three types of statutes are distinguished:

- The constitution itself, as the fundamental, supreme legal act;
- Separate constitutional statutes; and
- Ordinary statutes.

The class of constitutional statutes deserves our special attention. These statutes regulate relations and institutions of outstanding political and constitutional importance, such as the state organs, the relation of the state and social organizations, and basic rights. The negotiations among political groups during 1989 extended the subjects covered by constitutional acts, and revised the memory of an institution of Hungarian legal history, the "cardinal laws" (leges cardinales). Before 1949, those statutes were considered cardinal laws that regulated the fundamental institutions of the state and the basic principles of the (historical) constitution. In contrast to the constitutional practice of other countries, the enactment of Hungarian cardinal laws did not require any special procedure; they were passed by the same legislative procedure as other statutes.

The amended 1989 constitution has revived that institution, calling these statutes "acts of constitutional force," but for enacting them, just like for any amendment of the constitution, a two-thirds majority of votes is required. The amended constitution enumerates more than twenty subjects that should be regulated by an act of constitutional force, including among others the order of legislation, the legal status of members of parliaments, the list of ministries, and the detailed rules to be applied during a state of emergency.

But a problem has been created by Article 8, paragraph 2 of the constitution that sets up the following general rule: "Rules affecting fundamental rights and duties shall not be provided by legal rules other than Acts of constitutional force." This reflects the idea that fundamental rights should be guaranteed by a two-thirds majority of the parliament. This general provision extends greatly the range of the acts of constitutional force. It is not by change that two among the first four decisions of the Constitutional Court have concerned this rule.

In decision No. 3/1990 the Constitutional Court expressed its opinion that rules relating to the family and marriage affect fundamental rights and duties, so the modification of any provision of the Act on Family and Marriage requires a two-thirds majority. In another case, the constitutionality of a special tax was challenged. In its decision No. 5/1990 the Constitutional Court pronounced that rules imposing taxes on citizens affect fundamental duties, and their enactment requires a two-thirds majority. A two-thirds majority is not only a formal requirement but the proof of a broad consensus in the legislative body, so it is a constitutional guarantee. The Act on Credit Tax was passed by a majority of only 57.4 percent of the votes, so it did not fulfil the constitutional requirement. The court declared the act unconstitutional and annulled it.

As it stands, this provision of the constitution raises serious theoretical and practical difficulties for legislation, and a more precise delimination of the cases in which an act of constitutional force is really required would be desirable.

The Constitutional Court

The socialist theory of the state has denied the idea of the separation of powers, and consequently it has refused to admit the necessity of entrusting the protection of constitutionality to an independent organ like a constitutional court. In Hungary during the drafting of a new constitution it became obvious that a constitutional court should be a fundamental institution of the new political and legal system. The rules relating to a future constitutional court became a central issue in the negotiations among political groups. Contrary to the proposal of the Communist party, the opposition succeeded in considerably extending the court's competence. The Act No.

XXXII of 1989 on The Constitutional Court was enacted in October 1989, and soon afterwards the first five members of the court were elected by the parliament. (Five additional members will be elected after the general elections by the new parliament, while a third five members will be chosen during the fifth year subsequent to the creation of the court, so it will ultimately consist of fifteen judges.)

The judges of the court are elected for nine years, and they can be re-elected once. They cannot exercise any political activity, cannot be a member of any political party, and cannot make any political statement.

The most important competence of the Constitutional Court is the examination for unconstitutionality of legal rules after they are passed. Besides that the court's competence comprises:

- Constitutional review of yet not enacted bills;
- Examination of the conformity of legal rules with international treaties;
- Review of unconstitutional omission of legislation;
- The elimination of conflict of competences;
- The interpretation of the constitution; and
- Finally it deserves particular attention that anybody having been aggrieved as a result of the application of an unconstitutional law and having exhausted all of his legal remedies may have recourse to the court by submitting a constitutional complaint charging the violation of his constitutional rights.

The proceedings of the court can be initiated in general by an organ or a person entitled to do so, such as the parliament, the president of the republic, or the council of ministers. In two cases the court can proceed *ex officio* (conformity of legal rules with international treaties and review of unconstitutional omission of legislation), and in three cases on the initiative of *anybody* (repressive norm control, constitutional complaint, and unconstitutional omission of legislation). The decision of the court is final and without appeal, binding on everybody. If the Constitutional Court finds a legal norm unconstitutional, it declares it wholly or partly null and void.

An important, perhaps the principal function of the Constitutional Court is to protect civil liberties and other fundamental rights against government and, if necessary, against legislative action. The citizens of Hungary have even by international comparison a very wide-ranging possibility to appeal directly to the Constitutional Court. The court, through its decisions and interpretations, will strive to enforce and protect the widest possible range of human rights.

Democracy: A New Challenge?

While opening up a new prospect to realize human rights, recent political events also gave birth to new difficulties that Hungarian society has to face. The values of liberalism do not form an organic part of East European political culture; quite the contrary, the traditions of this part of Europe are rather lacking in these values. This fact can lead to a tension between individualistic western concepts of freedom and a more collectivistic approach to rights.

Socialist ideology has attached more importance to social and economic rights than to political and civil freedoms. The transformation of the economic system and the establishment of a market economy, worsened by the present economic crisis of the country, will inevitably result in a decline of social security and welfare services, and in a narrower comprehension of social rights. Therefore the historically well-known antinomy of equality (egalitarian values) and liberty (fundamental freedom) will strengthen.

A serious problem in eastern Europe is the condition of national minorities living outside their mother country. The Hungarian democratic opposition has always considered national minority rights as problems of human rights—the right to equality before the law, to promote their own culture, to the use of, and to be educated in their mother language, and "full opportunity for the actual enjoyment of human rights and fundamental freedoms" (VIIth Helsinki principle). The expectations that the historic turn of events in Czechoslovakia and in Romania would improve the condition of the Hungarian minorities have not been fulfilled. On the contrary, national hostilities and ethnic conflicts are gaining strength.

This account of unresolved problems shows that legal safeguards are not sufficient in themselves. The widespread practice of social tolerance will be required as well.

Chapter 16

Legal Safeguards for Human and Political Rights

Vojislav Stanovčić

In various member nations of the Conference on Security and Cooperation in Europe (CSCE) the main problem in the area of human rights and freedoms is not writing new standards in various CSCE follow-up meetings, but putting the various already ratified declarations and constitutional guarantees into practice and institutionalizing them. Implementation requires legal safeguards, i.e., introduction of legal principles, provisions, and procedures which can give real life to international covenants and conventions and to some general tenets and achievements of democratic civilization in this field.

We have to realize that turning international declarations into consitutional provisions and statutes is not enough in countries where constitutions have long been treated as mere noncompulsory promises by those in power, as instruments of power seekers and gifts from rulers to their subjects—and where citizens regard constitutions as just "pieces of paper." This essay will therefore first discuss some preconditions for successful implementation of legal provisions before going on to legal safeguards as such. The particular barriers in most East European countries include: (1) the lack of democratic tradition and institutions; (2) prevailing authoritarian patterns of political behavior, usually colored by vehement and intolerant nationalism; (3) the lack of civil society; and (4) many deeply rooted oligarchic or bureaucratic interest and ideological rationalizations which interfere with the rule of law. Preconditions for higher standards of human rights certainly include a developed civil society, an adequate political culture, and democratic institutions.

This may sound like the long way around, but many East European lawyers, scholars, intellectuals, and politicians, moved by a new spirit, are already advocating and trying to introduce and implement proper legal safeguards and standards. The idea of the rule of law, for example, finds increasing circulation (even if it often takes the not very promising form of *Rechtsstaat*). Due process of law is also advocated—although such nice legal formulations have often been just a facade for authoritarian politics. Throughout eastern Europe, with only a few exceptions, there is a sharp discrepancy between legal norms and reality. As one experienced lawyer and historian commented, the worst thing is not the rigidity and nonrationality of the law in force, but the fact that according to that law everything could become legal if person A says it is legal, or illegal if the same person says so. And person A is not somebody high ranking, but an anonymous official. Law has typically been envisaged as an instrument of political power at all levels; most recently such arbitrary power has sprung from the assumed role of the party in society and has been disguised by many ideological rationalizations.

Some standards of human rights and freedoms have to be taken as criteria in assessing political systems. The human rights approach to classifying them is a relatively new one, but it is gaining ground simply because this is such an essential feature of a democratic political system. While some anthropological and ethical arguments and reasoning were used in the past in favor of human freedom, human rights and freedoms have been treated since the eighteenth century as a condition for human emancipation and social and economic development. And today it is justly stressed that basic human rights are essential for safeguarding international peace and security. But even if human rights are accepted as nominal yardsticks for political systems, we should bear in mind that it is a long road from declaring rights to realizing them in practice.

The relationships between individuals and institutionalized political power, i.e., state governments, are the basic political relationship reflected in constitutions and in what we call today basic human rights. In one way or another the position of an individual in relation to political power is reflected in the oldest works of literature, histories, and philosophical treatises, from Aeschylus' *Prometheus Bound* to Sophocles' *Antigone*. In his treatises Cicero asked whether one should obey an unjust law which is contrary to natural law; medieval scholars held long discussions about whether an order of natural and moral law is above positive law, and these discussions continue to the present day. Today a contemporary German legal theorist, Gustav Radbruch, who began as a positivist in the theory of law, has concluded that we have a duty to resist injust laws—to oppose legal unjustice in the name of the justice which stands above positive law.

Similar discussions are also going on now in communist countries where an established, "positive" legal order has to be replaced by one which is more in accord with principles of democratic civilization. Introducing safeguards to human rights will serve the purpose only if the whole legal environment improves.

The Universal Declaration of Human Rights (1948), the UN Charter for the equality of men and the expansion of basic freedoms, and the Atlantic Charter statement of war aims were all based on the modern liberalism that developed from the seventeenth through the nineteenth centuries. A key element of this liberalism was constitutionalism to limit political power and guarantee basic rights to individuals. These ideas in turn had their roots in theories of natural law and social compact conceived in ancient Greece. Their antithesis was the absolute power which appeared in the twentieth century, i.e., totalitarian power. Human rights and freedoms cannot be secure under absolute, i.e., unlimited power.

Modern constitutionalism sets three limits on power. The first is basic human rights (as advocated, e.g., in Locke's concept of government by consent of those governed, and, a century earlier, by Bodin's realization that fundamental laws and respect for private property limit the power of the king to a certain degree). The second is rule of law instead of arbitrary will ("The rule of law, not of man"). Today the holder of absolute power is in principle the monopoly party; in practice, however, the holder frequently is the party leader. As Robert Michels phrased it, "Le Party, c'est moi." The third limit, separation of powers—or, in the American version "checks and balances"—was added by Locke, Montesquieu, and the American Founding Fathers on the assumption that absolute, unlimited power is an evil and that only power checks power.

The pioneering role in human rights and separation of powers was played by the Declaration of Independence of July 4, 1776, and the French Declaration of the Rights of Man and Citizen of August 26, 1789. The Virginia Bill of Rights (June 12, 1776) and the Constitution of Virginia (June 29, 1776), as well as some other states' constitutions; Jefferson's *Notes on Virginia, The Federalist Papers,* and the U.S. Constitution itself played an enormous role. But the Declaration of Independence laid the cornerstone for government based on "self-evident and unalienable rights" and the right of the people to institute government, "laying its foundation on such principles and organizing its powers in such a form as to them shall seem most likely to effect their safety and happiness." We should try to lay foundations of East European governments on these eighteenth-century principles of freedom and reason.

The French Declaration stated something that sounds very modern: that ignorance, forgetfulness, or contempt of the rights of man are the sole causes of public misfortunes and corruptions of governments. It also subscribed to the natural, unalienable, and sacred rights of man, and in Article 16 said that any society in which the guarantee of the rights is not assured or the separation of powers not determined has no constitution.

Nonetheless, it took about a century before those promised rights became reality. Not until 1946 did the Declaration became part of the French Constitution. The American (federal government with dispersed power) and the French (Jacobin type of government) way of safeguarding human rights were different. The authoritarian tradition of eastern Europe is closer to French experience, but many intellectuals are aware of the importance of these differences.

Most modern constitutions have a separate chapter dedicated to human rights, freedoms, and duties; the Yugoslav Constitution has fifty articles on civil rights. Reality often belies these fine words, however, as can be seen by contrasting the Soviet Constitution of 1936 with the show trials of 1937/38.

In *The Federalist Papers* Alexander Hamilton argued that separation of powers and other institutional arrangements (impeachment, habeas corpus, trial by jury, no "bill of attainder or ex post facto law," etc.) would serve the purpose much better than a bill of rights. The latter, he said, "would sound much better in a treatise of ethics than in a constitution of government." His main argument was that the very structure of the Constitution guarantees human rights better than any declaration.

Some advocates of human rights in eastern Europe today combine this approach to structure with an explicit declaration of rights. Some Yugoslav lawyers also pay close attention to the American Bill of Rights (1791) on limiting basic freedoms— a practice that is common all over Europe. These lawyers now argue that constitutions should simply forbid enacting any law in some fields, such as freedom of speech and of the press.

The Rule of Law

In Yugoslavia, the Soviet Union, Hungary, Poland, and some other East European countries, the idea of the *Rechtsstaat* is the cry of the day. To some extent it can be taken as a hope and a safeguard for human rights. The term ("Pravna drzava," "pravovoe gosudarstvo") cannot be translated literally as "legal state," but it means much less than the idea of the rule of law. To achieve the nineteenth-century German idea of the *Rechtsstaat* would certainly be a great step forward from an authoritarian party rule which sees law as an instrument of its power rather than a limitation on it.

But there is another misconception here. It is often wrongly assumed that the *Rechtsstaat* would be realized if present-day laws were entirely implemented. Yet the quality of present-day laws is so low that their implementation could not lead to the *Rechtsstaat*, let alone to the rule of law.

Instead, virtually the whole legal system in East European countries has to be changed. *Rechtsstaat* or legality in the sense of Max Weber implies rationality of laws, and that rationality is missing in many laws in eastern Europe. Moreover, one may do only what is explicitly permitted, in the way permitted. On such a premise—and given the preoccupation with the strict social control—complicated nets of legal provisions have been created that are obstacles to normal communications and trade in these societies.

In addition, the very idea of the rule of law contradicts the role reserved for the Communist party, with its monopoly on power. Because of the monopolistic position, that power became absolute, unlimited, irresponsible. It was never exposed to any free elections. Therefore the party state or ideological state has to be transformed into a lay state which will be free from ideology. The party's monopolistic and privileged position needs to be broken.

Total control of the socialist state relies on a rigid, elaborated, and extremely diversified legal system. In the most essential questions, such norms can be arbitrarily interpreted by some members or bodies of the party oligarchy and/or government bureaucracies. It is widely known that it would be helpful to abolish the influence of arbitrary political will, but it is less well known that the whole legal system is an irrational obstacle created to strengthen state control.

On this issue different societies have very different ideas. Even Mikhail Gorbachev declared that the new principle will be introduced of allowing everything that is not explicitly and for good reason forbidden by law. This idea, which is popular in Poland and Yugoslavia, would turn the role of law upside down: from an instrument of ideologically determined social control to an instrument of problem- and conflict-solving.

As an instrument of social control the legal system is full of vague provisions which can be interpreted arbitrarily. There is bureaucratic resistance to removing such provisions.

There have been many cases of countries with written constitutions listing many rights and freedoms—and at the same time prisons for people who try to practice those rights. So there are "constitutions" in name without constitutionalism, as well as nations with many laws but still without legality or even less legitimacy. Also, certain rights can be guaranteed by a constitution with a provision that the matter will be further regulated in detail by follow-up laws. And then by such laws these rights are limited so that nothing remains of the constitutional "guarantees."

There are many declarations which praise the citizen, usually as "a worker"—then in reality deprive him of the possibility of influencing the government. The ancient Greeks used to divide all citizens into *polites*, i.e., those who participated in the electing and work of government, and *idiotes* who were deprived of these rights. We could say that in socialist states inhabitants were for several decades treated by governments as *idiotes*. Direct free elections with multiple alternative candidates proposed and supported by different political parties is one condition for the safeguarding and improvement of human rights.

Pluralism and autonomous civil society are equally important safeguards of human rights. Autonomous economic, cultural, political associations, enterprises, and trade unions; and a free press (uninfluenced by the government or by the single party) allow citizens to be relatively independent from the government in their earnings. Ownership of property is among those fundamental rights which used to be treated as inalienable rights. Even Jean Bodin, who introduced the term "sovereignty," realized that the right of ownership of private property limits sovereign and absolute power. It also supports implementation of some other rights and is instrumental in achieving autonomy.

In another sense pluralism means a multiparty system. That implies political opposition, some political fair play and parliamentary rules, and criticism of government in parliament and in the press. This is perhaps the best single safeguard of human rights.

On such pluralistic grounds an autonomous civil society appears which is not totally controlled by the government but limits any government to fulfilling functions stated precisely by the constitution. In all East European countries, including the Soviet Union, civil society either did not exist or was not saved (except, in some countries, for the church) as everything was put under the political control of the party state. There is much interest in eastern Europe now in the phenomenon of civil society; as one example Feodor Burlatsky, one of Gorbachev's counselors, said at the International Political Science Association Congress in Washington in 1988 that the first task in the Soviet Union is to establish civil society.

To "establish civil society" is certainly not a matter of decision, but of letting social, economic, political, and cultural processes develop freely, without rigid control, but in the framework of law. This implies separation of party and state to make the state (and bureaucracy) ideologically neutral.

Procedural Guarantees and Due Process

Some specifically legal safeguards include certain principles, provisions, and procedures that cannot be formulated or implemented in a schematic way, since implementation in different social milieus gives different results. For example, the jury system as a democratic safeguard in the judiciary system would probably weaken rather than strengthen legal guarantees in an authoritarian political culture. Mass populist movements favor a type of government which subdues and dominates the judiciary.

Such principles as the old Roman *audiatur et altera pars* or *audire alteram partem* (listen to the other side) and many other similar principles (*nullum crimen*, presumption of innocence) need to permeate the legal system. There are some procedural guarantees which in one way or another secure civilized standards. For example, the summary trial and particularly summary execution even of the worst criminals violate the normal legal procedure. Due process of law implies some time schedule to the right to defend oneself, privilege against self-incrimination, i.e., a right to refuse to answer a question or give testimony against oneself (the Fifth Amendment in the U.S. Constitution). Right of appeal goes together with the principle of review by a higher court.

Transformation from a party ideological state to a *Rechtsstaat* and from the rule of political will to rule of law is probably a long-term process. But if successful, it will create conditions more favorable to human rights. Rights and freedoms should be treated as basic social values and as a rule should be stated directly in the basic constitutional provisions, with a prohibition on laws restricting these rights by "interpreting" them or elaborating details.

The separation of powers, including an independent judiciary, is essential. In eastern Europe, however, the more usual government is a Jacobin one based on "unity of power." In such a system judges are elected for a finite time and can be recalled by local or higher authorities. In such a system judges have to behave according to the expectations of those who elected them. Judges should instead be elected and should hold their offices during good behavior.

The constitution must ban laws that limit or abolish those rights guaranteed by constitutions. All restrictions (in cases of invasion or rebellion) should be regulated by the constitution and not left to be decided by different bodies or administrations. If some limits have to be imposed—because of new international covenants; violent change of the constitutional order; propagation of war; instigation of national, religious, or racial hatred and intolerance; threatening of public order or public morality—such limits should be narrowly interpreted. Habeas corpus can contribute greatly to avoiding misinterpretations or violations.

Constitutions should specify the obligatory implementation of ratified international covenants and conventions. But sometimes even this does not help. The Yugoslav Constitution of 1974, Article 210, provides that courts directly apply international conventions which are publicized (and we have to assume that publicized means signed and ratified). But in practice many problems appear concerning the implementation of international contracts. During the work on the proposal of the new constitution submitted by the Presidency of the State of Yugoslavia quite a wide consensus was reached that West European standards in the field of human rights (including the European Convention of 1950 and the Optional Protocol of the International Covenant on Civil and Political Rights of 1966) should be respected and incorporated into the new Yugoslav constitution.

The real problem is how to make adopted declarations obligatory in terms of domestic law. It is an even more complicated task to secure implementation of general principles or documents which some countries did not sign. It would be useful to prepare a more detailed Codex based on the Universal Declaration, a Codex which eventually would be accepted by many more states. Of course, the International Covenants on Civil and Political Rights and on Economic, Social, and Cultural Rights (both of December 16, 1966) already incorporated many principles of the Universal Declaration.

Due process of law is very important, but there is no definitive answer as to what this includes or excludes. Of course, secret trials, extorted confessions, biased attitudes toward defense witnesses, vague accusations, short periods of time given to lawyers to prepare a defense, no possibility of appeal, and executions immediately after the verdict is pronounced indicate lack of proper procedure.

Many procedural principles could be taken as part of due process and a contribution to human rights safeguards. The right of an accused or arrested to a lawyer in all phases of the procedure is essential for getting proper legal assistance. Introduction of such a possibility would be of great help in improving the human rights situation.

Indeterminate sentences, which do not specify the exact amount of time to be served in prison, and which are legally possible even in the United States, contribute very much to legal uncertainty. The role of procedural guarantees regarding the time, appeals, rights in the process, terms, and conditions of trial which are parts of criminal procedure are in most cases regulated in accordance with modern democratic standards, but malpractice is widespread, and certainly many improvements could be made. But fewer changes are expected in criminal procedure than in what is called "material criminal law." For example, the Criminal Code is in the process of being changed in Yugoslavia. Some articles dealing with *verbal delicts* are to be abolished and some others restricted and clarified in meaning, because so-called legal standards are vague and indetermined, e.g., what do "enemy propaganda" or "hostile demonstration" or "violent" mean? Even terrorism is too widely and too vaguely used; such qualifications have to be defined in terms of acts, not by alleged intentions or on the basis of some constructed assumptions.

Onus probandi (the burden of proof), i.e., responsibility to prove something, must rest on the one who states or assumes something. Yet one public prosecutor said in a criminal case that it would be difficult for the accused to prove that he did not commit the crime. And in Yugoslavia people accused of "unjustified enrichment" (illegal accumulation of wealth) often have to prove their innocence.

Such basic freedoms as freedom of the press, freedom of assembly, and freedom of association are not only freedoms per se, but instrumental in safeguarding other rights and freedoms. These should be pronounced as constitutional principles of CSCE participating states. Some kind of Cases Register should also be established.

Legal provisions concerning churches and religious freedoms tend to be more flexible and liberal now in eastern Europe and Yugoslavia, but many problems from property to educational institutions remain to be properly settled. Conscientious objectors should be protected in a certain way and offered the possibility of serving in noncombat units or something similar, but usually there is resistance to giving them a privileged position.

There are two institutional devices which play an enormous role in protecting human rights against violations by government machinery and administration: (1) constitutional courts and, (2) administrative dispute. Judicial review over constitutionality of laws and decrees had been rejected in all socialist states on the ground that government bodies can never adopt an unconstitutional statue or decree because it is their role and duty to guard constitutionality and legality! The first constitutional court in a socialist country was established in Yugoslavia in 1953; another was established in Hungary, and one is under consideration in Poland.

The Yugoslav constitutional courts prove that this is an institution which really helps safeguard human rights, declaring many laws and administrative decrees unconstitutional on the grounds that they limit or violate constitutionally guaranteed rights and freedoms. There is a widely supported request that constitutional courts be given jurisdiction over all matters concerning (political) human rights and disputes over the legal status of political parties.

In an administrative dispute a citizen can sue a government body (usually an administrative unit) in a regular court to address the alleged violation of a law or a citizen's right by misapplying law. Before this possibility was introduced, a citizen could appeal only to a higher administrative organ; as a rule, the decision would be in favor of the lower bureaucratic body.

On the basis of Yugoslav experience some further suggestions can be made for amending the constitution. The discretionary power of state administration is too wide and should be reduced. The new Yugoslav constitution should abolish discrimination on ideological grounds, or on the basis of political beliefs. Efforts in this direction have so far failed except in declaring "social and political suitableness" as unconstitutional. In the current constitution of 1974 there are many clauses which refer to working people and citizens. This is taken as discrimination, because some political rights (voting for certain bodies) are conditioned on being employed. Many lawyers and Yugoslav Human Rights Forum members also think that habeus corpus is violated by such provisions as the so-called isolation of individuals labeled as menaces to public order without specific accusations, and the acceptance of retroactive status in the "interests of socialist society" or "if general interest requires." Unfortunately, even if prohibitions are enacted in the constitution, the Yugoslav federal structure means that federal constitutional provisions can be limited by republics and provinces.

Freedom of enterprise and self-employment is very important in allowing economic and general autonomy, which is especially important for exercising political rights. These should be supplemented by protection from agencies knowing facts about personal life. Also there should be a right of correction of printed matter obliging the state to give a right to answer on the grounds of *audiatur et altera pars*.

One of the issues not only in Yugoslavia, but also in the Soviet Union and possibly in Czechoslovakia and Romania, will be the scope and the nature of the right to self-determination. It is provided for in several international covenants. But such provisions have to be interpreted in connection with other relevant provisions like Articles III and IV of the Helsinki Final Act, which deal with inviolability of the frontiers and territorial integrity of states, respectively. These provisions could contradict each other. The same contradicting principles are to be found in the Declaration on the Inadmissibility of Intervention in the Domestic Affairs of States and the Protection of Their Independence and Sovereignty. It seems that the right of self-determination cannot be realized on account of territorial integrity and secure borders, and so it does not imply the right to secession.

Institutionalization of democratic elections is of primary importance for human rights. To secure to citizens the status of political subjects in the fullest sense will have effects on their situation concerning human rights. Democratization implies political pluralism, separation of powers, genuine federalism in a multinational state, *Rechtsstaat*, and an independent judiciary—all of which increase the possibility of realizing human rights. But in a multinational and federal state like Yugoslavia these institutional characteristics are associated with the federal judiciary. It has to be in a position to protect basic rights and freedoms of citizens if violated by actions of governments of federal units. That is not the case now in Yugoslavia. And it is not likely that component units will be ready to invest such power in federal courts. To declare punishable all acts which violate human rights and freedoms would secure their better protection. And even more appropriate to serve this function could be the institution of some kind of "ombudsman" who would take care of and be of assistance to citizens in protecting their constitutional rights. In the course of constitutional and legal changes in instituting a multiparty system, the party monopoly is likely to be removed.

Civic culture of a democratic type is one of the prerequisites for proper safeguarding of human rights. Courses on human rights should be included in the educational curriculum.

Constitutional changes, if adopted, could considerably improve human rights in Yugoslavia. Two proposals submitted to the Federal Assembly in 1990 aim to introduce pluralism of ownership (mixed and market economy) political and (multiparty) pluralism, and to treat human rights as the basis of the constitutional system. The current crises and tensions between nationalities tend toward autarky and closed national states and economies, however, and are not favorable to improvement in human rights. The Latin saying that *inter arma silent muse* could *mutatis mutandis* refer not only to muse but also to human rights.

Commentary

The discussion of the broad range of issues involved in the CSCE basket III revolved around the problems that the countries of eastern Europe would have in adapting their political and legal systems to accept the full range of human and political rights that were already guaranteed in western Europe. Ambassador Kampelman posed several questions and engaged in discussion with Professor Stanovčić concerning the need for the introduction of guarantees of the rule of law in countries like Yugoslavia. The United States, Kampelman pointed out, has as one of its goals in the forthcoming CSCE Conference on the Human Dimension the development and adoption by the CSCE countries of provisions leading to such a rule of law guarantee.

In commenting on the two papers in this session, Koenraad Lenaerts, Professor of European Law at the University of Leuven and a judge on the Court of First Instance of the European Communities in Luxembourg, focused upon the very different approaches taken by authoritarian societies and democratic societies in dealing with basic economic, political, and human rights. Lenaerts fully agreed that there was a need for a guarantee for the rule of law, but even so, wide disparities would remain. He pointed out that even within democratic societies, there is a wide variation in the accepted role of government in the economy (just compare the United States with France) and the level of basic assured rights in areas such as long-term unemployment insurance, health care, and access to higher education.

Referring to the European Court of Human Rights, Lenaerts pointed out that under the system adopted by the Council of Europe, all persons under the jurisdiction of a government that is a member of the Council, even if they are not a citizen, can sue that government in a supranational court (European Court of Human Rights) after they have exhausted all of their local legal remedies. He cited a case in which a citizen of Belgium sued the government of Belgium for having an inheritance law that discriminated against illegitimate children. The claimant won the case and now all of the members of the Council of Europe have to provide equal inheritance rights to children born within wedlock and without.

V. The Helsinki Process

Chapter 17

The Conference on Security and Cooperation in Europe and the Future of Europe

Speech delivered at the Woodrow Wilson International Center for Scholars by Rep. Steny Hoyer, Co-Chairman, U.S. Commission on Security and Cooperation in Europe, April 23, 1990

I have been working with the Helsinki Commission for five years, both as Chairman and Co-Chairman. When I first joined the Commission, the Conference on Security and Co-operation in Europe (CSCE) had hit a sort of mid-life crisis. The big question on everyone's minds on the eve of the Vienna Review Meeting was whether the Helsinki process was credible: had we not handed the Soviets a victory and gotten very little in return? Had the process not emphasized security at the expense of human rights? Was it not time to withdraw from the Helsinki process?

I have heard no suggestion that the United States leave the CSCE in recent months. Instead, in the wake of the stunning events we have witnessed in Europe over the past year, I have learned to field questions like: "Do you have to find a new job now?" Questions like this reflect a sense that the Helsinki process has fulfilled its mandate. My response is that our work has been successful to date, but it is by no means over. The CSCE's mission is varied and changing, and our responsibility is to make sure the process can rise to each new challenge. One of the starkest challenges is, in the words of the old civil rights song, to "keep our eyes on the prize." The CSCE's first contribution was to set high standards in international relations and, most important, in relations between citizens and states.

But standards are not achievements. Human rights guarantees are by no means a *fait accompli* in a number of CSCE countries. And the kinds of tensions that are coming to the fore in the Soviet Union and eastern Europe—tensions that may have been swept under the rug for years—present a nagging threat to the human rights advances the peoples of the region have won.

During the Vienna Review Meeting, I proposed that our preeminent goal in the CSCE should be the "zero option" in human rights: zero political prisoners; zero divided spouses; zero divided families; zero refusals to requests to emigrate or to return; zero broadcasts jammed; zero restraints on religious observance and teaching; zero curbs on the right to communicate, to assemble, to organize into free association; zero national efforts to undermine cultural identities of minorities. We have come a long way to achieving the zero option in human rights—but we are not there yet.

I have just returned from a Helsinki Commission trip with Chairman Dennis DeConcini to Yugoslavia, Romania, and Bulgaria. I would suggest a similar trip to anyone who thinks that the Helsinki process has achieved its goals.

The Balkans is an area racked by interethnic tensions, where the human rights progress achieved to date is fragile and subject to fast erosion. In the past, some have tended to write off the problems of the Balkans as intractable, a tragic legacy of centuries of strife. The Balkans was the crucible of this century's first war in Europe, the famous "tinderbox" that threatened to destabilize the security of Europe then and now. The region is an ideal place to test the potential of the Helsinki process. The people of Yugoslavia, Romania, and Bulgaria are uncertain about their future, but full of hope— hope that they, too, can meet the high standards set in Helsinki and Vienna. The engines of that hope are the round table talks that, beginning in Poland in April 1988 and taking place throughout Central and eastern Europe into this year, have hammered out the mechanics of that region's long-awaited transition to democracy. In the past few weeks they have made their Balkan debut.

These round table talks have brought one-time prisoners into negotiations with their jailers. They have brought independent parties to talks with the rulers who have held a political monopoly for years. And they have the potential to sit neighbors down with neighbors to discuss the charges that have flown back and forth and past each other for decades. They offer the best prospects for addressing the sometimes conflicting needs of minority and majority populations, and solving the problems that threaten to sink eastern and Central Europe's fledgling democracies.

Two weeks ago, an independent human rights advocacy group brought Serbs and Albanians together for the first time to discuss their feelings about Kosovo, the province of the Serbian Republic where members of the two groups live in an uneasy and often interrupted truce. The talks proceeded haltingly, reflecting a years-long unwillingness on each side even to enter into a discussion with the other. Talks have begun also in the Transylvanian town of Tirgu Mures, where increasing tension over the Hungarian minority's attempts to regain its eroded cultural rights exploded in violent clashes last month.

The talks mirror the dynamic that has been shaping Europe's progress for fifteen years: the Helsinki process, a round table writ large. Since 1975, one function of that process has been to provide a sounding board for nations to express concerns about one another. It is a model for members of vying communities to enter into talks, and it offers a potential to facilitate those discussions. Everyone we asked in Yugoslavia, Romania, and Bulgaria credited the CSCE with playing a critical role in the revolutions of the last year. Lech Wałesa and Václav Havel made similar observations in their speeches to joint sessions of Congress. The process has worked so well, in fact, that I believe we should consider proposing a similar conference for other areas of the world, like Latin America, Asia, and Africa.

The talks taking place now in the three Balkan countries we visited point up the value of placing a renewed emphasis on conflict resolution in the CSCE context. An often overlooked principle in the Helsinki Final Act calls for the participating states to ''use such means as negotiation, enquiry, mediation, conciliation, arbitration, judicial settlement or other peaceful means of their own choice'' to settle disputes. We have reached a point in the process when this principle is viable and very useful, as Prime Minister Thatcher pointed out recently.

I have an instinctive bias against institutionalizing the Helsinki process. Much of the strength of that process has stemmed from its flexibility, and that flexibility in turn has grown out of its lack of bureaucracy. But if we are to develop the CSCE mandate to settle disputes peacefully, some institutionalization may well be necessary. I would urge that consideration be given to the creation of a permanent CSCE mediation council to work with both states and peoples in conflict. This CSCE mediation council should supplement, rather than replace, existing dispute resolution institutions. Its mandate could include mediation of internal disputes with the concurrence of the state in question, and could be particularly useful in the case of disputes between ethnic groups, such as those in Transylvania and Kosovo.

Only through a dynamic institution such as the CSCE will we be able to grapple with a changing Europe, especially as new and complex issues come to the fore. Let us consider just one change in the making. For many years CSCE discussions reverberated between two different concepts of rights: the western emphasis on civil and political rights, on the one hand, and the Soviet emphasis on socioeconomic rights. We argued endlessly about the equivalency or lack thereof between the two types of rights. Now this dichotomy between the conflicting concepts and application of rights seems to be fading.

Yet a new conflict is rearing its head. Today the traditional American emphasis on individual rights is coming up against the newly resurgent call for the recognition of and respect for national rights—an idea that makes many in this country uncomfortable, but which we must face squarely and honestly. How these two kinds of rights will be balanced remains an open and troubling question.

The CSCE as an institution, as a process, and in the persons of its members, increasingly will have to address the relationship between these kinds of rights and try to harmonize the inherent conflicts between them. Ultimately, a decisive criterion of the process' success in a fluid environment is how well it copes with such potentially explosive issues.

In addition to concentrating more on the peaceful settlement of disputes, I would urge that we continue to develop the verification the CSCE has built into processes that all too often have been obscured or hidden. This has been most evident in the security sphere. The 1986 Stockholm Document was an essential stepping-stone to the Intermediate-range Nuclear Forces (INF) Treaty signed less than two years later and to subsequent negotiations still in progress, such as the conference on conventional arms reductions.

Last June, on behalf of the U.S. delegation to the Paris meeting of the CSCE Conference on the Human Dimension, I introduced a proposal to make free and fair elections a CSCE standard. At the time, that proposal was considered premature. Now the countries of eastern Europe are holding free elections for the first time in 40 or more years and are inviting observers from other CSCE states. They are extending the principle of on-site verification used to good advantage in the military sphere to the political realm.

Hope tempered with realism—this is what drives the Helsinki process, and makes it such a tempting framework on which to build the future of Europe. Our task now is not to get carried away with our hopes, and overburden the process with a much-enlarged mandate and accelerated timetable. At the same time, let us not permit a fear of seeing our leading role in Europe eroded serve as a brake on the process. Indeed, our very reluctance may lead to this erosion.

Over the past few months, the Bush administration has moved from a semisuspicious attitude toward the CSCE to one of proclaiming the Helsinki process as a "pillar" of U.S. policy in Europe. The administration has declared that it wants the United States to play a major role in the Helsinki process, yet practical steps to pursue this policy are somewhat lagging given the tremendous speed with which events are changing in Europe. The commission believes that the administration's tentative response to Soviet President Gorbachev's December proposal of a second CSCE summit runs the risk of having the United States be perceived as a hesitant participant in building Europe's future—a perception that is clearly incorrect.

By now a Helsinki summit in late 1990 seems to have universal endorsement, even if different states have varying ideas about the mandate and scope of the meeting. The Soviets see the summit primarily as a means to get an international handle on a reunified Germany. The Germans see it as a vehicle to achieve European approval on their reunification process. The United States sees a summit largely in terms of approving a treaty on conventional military forces. Other CSCE states see it as the focal point for launching of bold initiatives to create a new European architecture.

And there are points of substantial agreement on the next Helsinki summit, all based on the strengths the process has demonstrated over the years. First, most states agree that consensus should remain the operational principle for decision making within the CSCE. Second, there is general agreement that the regularity, frequency, and level of political consultations among the CSCE states should be maintained. Third, most participating states view the summit as an opportunity to explore new CSCE initiatives rather than to launch such initiatives. These points of substantial agreement represent significant starting points in determining the future course of the Helsinki process. Like Prime Minister Thatcher's suggestions late last month, these ideas continue in substantially the same direction as we have charted already in the CSCE.

The United States should continue to act like the full member of the CSCE it is and offer to host this year's summit or another major meeting. The Helsinki Commission made this proposal fully one month ago and is disappointed that no answer has been forthcoming yet. The Commission believes that the United States has a continuing valuable role to play within Europe and within CSCE, and while some in the United States fear the worst from European economic integration, imagining that this country would be shut out of "Fortress Europe," the newly emerging Europe could prove to offer opportunities to develop even closer political ties with the United States.

Similar fears center around the U.S. role in European security. But there is no need for the administration to be defensive about the future of the North Atlantic Treaty Organization (NATO) in response to the proposals for a European security system under the CSCE. The CSCE has complemented NATO. In fact, NATO cooperation, as a guarantor of European peace and security, has been strengthened by the CSCE process.

Compromises will have to be made in the development of all phases of a new European system. Yet there is no reason for NATO to have to disappear. In fact, NATO and a continuing U.S. presence in Europe have support from many quarters.

With inspired leadership, both can play a nurturing and strengthening role as new institutions are being built in Europe—and as we continue to work as a full partner in the CSCE, a process to which we have contributed from the beginning and from which we will continue to benefit well into the future.

Chapter 18

Concluding Thoughts

Samuel F. Wells, Jr.

In the six months since December 1989, when planning began for the conference that produced this volume, the answers to many of the questions about the future of Europe have begun—however dimly—to take shape. Government officials and academic specialists in western Europe and the United States are in general agreement about the major elements of an emerging new system of political, economic, and security institutions for the new Europe.

The pace of German unification has clearly driven many of these choices. The central actors were the people of the German Democratic Republic who expressed an overwhelming desire to improve their political and economic condition and Chancellor Helmut Kohl, who saw an opportunity to achieve rapid unification of his nation at the same time that he was positioning his party for a likely victory in all-German elections that will now be held before the end of 1990. George Bush and James Baker also played major roles in maintaining frequent and detailed contact with their counterparts in the Federal Republic of Germany in order to support and guide, and occasionally to reinforce, the rapid development of West German policy. The Bush administration worked hard to consult frequently with the leaders of the United Kingdom and France as well as with Mikhail Gorbachev and Eduard Shevardnadze to win their support for the policy choices that were being shaped largely in Bonn.

The Soviet and American leaders outlined the basic components of a solution to the German question at the Washington summit of May 30–June 3, 1990, and the two German states began the process of implementing this arrangement when the legislatures of the Federal Republic of Germany and the German Democratic Republic passed identical pledges on June 21, 1990, to guarantee Poland's present borders in treaty form after unification was completed. Chancellor Kohl also called on the members of North Atlantic Treaty Organization (NATO) to join with the members of the Warsaw Pact in adopting a nonaggression pact within the Conference on Security and Cooperation in Europe (CSCE) framework as a means of reassuring the Soviet Union that it has nothing to fear from a unified Germany. A major step was taken on July 16, 1990, when the Soviet Union announced its acceptance of a unified Germany belonging to NATO.

A skeletal description of the new European system as it appears at the end of July 1990 would include these elements:

- A unified Germany within NATO with certain assurances being given to Germany's neighbors and to the Soviet Union as are basically outlined in the nine points President Bush presented to Gorbachev at the Washington summit;
- A European Community completing its economic integration at an accelerating rate with monetary union soon to follow and some limited steps toward political union to come probably within two more years;
- The United States continuing to play a significant role in Europe with substantial political, economic, and military dimensions including a troop presence gradually reduced to about 75,000 after the second agreement on Conventional Forces in Europe;
- The Soviet Union with a continuing valid security interest in the new European system and possessing, as its only instrument of power, the most powerful military force in Europe built around a potent nuclear arsenal;
- NATO continuing with lower force levels and with probably a significant change in doctrine and structure in order to adjust to the new circumstances in Europe. In the likely event of successful conventional arms reductions, the possibility of a short-warning attack on western Europe will no longer exist;
- The nations of eastern Europe seeking closer ties with the West and proceeding at different rates, and with different degrees of success, toward pluralist political democracy and with mixed economies combining some market principles

with continued state sectors. Eastern Europe will show even more clearly than at present its division into two groups: Central Europe (Poland, Czechoslovakia, and Hungary) will move unevenly toward political and economic democracy, while southeastern Europe (Yugoslavia, Bulgaria, and Romania) will face greater political and economic problems compounded by ethnic conflicts;

- The nations of eastern Europe will begin to establish links to the West before their reform and democratization are completed. These links will first be through the Council of Europe and later through some form of associate membership in the European Community;

- The members of the European Free Trade Association (EFTA) will become associated with the European Community through the negotiations on European Economic Space (EES), but the European Community will not accept any more full members until after it completes the implementation of the single market and the currency and monetary union among its twelve present members and makes some decision on political union;

- A shifting mixture of evolving European regional organizations will continue for some years. The nature of the structure of the European Community is unclear, because the Germans want a federal Europe with greater centralization than the French, who prefer a confederation of basically sovereign states. The British, for their part, are even less willing than the French to delegate sovereignty to European institutions. Along with the European Community, EFTA, the Council of Europe, CSCE, and NATO, there may be other groupings formed among the nations of Central and Southeastern Europe.

- The CSCE will exercise a larger role in security, economic, and political affairs than it has in the past.

The nature of the expanded role of the CSCE is not as widely accepted or understood as most of the other elements of the new system. There are a number of proposals for the CSCE to become the major security organization for Europe. The Soviet delegation brought such a proposal to the Washington summit, although it received very little discussion. Some normally well-informed, prudent pundits such as Charles Krauthammer have proposed that the CSCE be transformed into "the European League" in order to win Soviet approval of a unified Germany belonging to NATO.[1] These proposals ask too much of the CSCE and if accepted could become counterproductive by making the Helsinki process into a club dominated by the major states and thereby removing the qualities so valuable to the neutral states and the vulnerable nations of eastern Europe.

Among the small group of political leaders and diplomats who have significant experience with the CSCE, there is a general consensus about what the CSCE should be asked to do. The Helsinki process should be kept, in the opinion of these experienced specialists, as a process with minimal institutional characteristics beyond the creation of a small secretariat. These specialists tend to agree that the unanimous voting procedure should be retained because of its widespread and enthusiastic acceptance among the smaller states. Given its limited institutional quality and its lengthy and often inconclusive procedures, the CSCE cannot be a security guarantor, nor is it desirable to identify a smaller group to function on behalf of all thirty-five as something on the order of a "European Security Council."

But there are many new and expanded tasks that the CSCE can be structured to handle, and these include:

- Expanding development of confidence- and security-building measures;
- Providing verification for arms control agreements;
- Providing crisis prevention teams and peacekeeping units for regional and national minority disputes;
- Serving as a forum for the political resolution of disputes;
- Ensuring the collective rights of national minorities;
- Assisting in the introduction of market principles and mechanisms into former command economies;
- Guaranteeing human rights in a more comprehensive manner; and
- Setting standards for free elections and the rule of law in all member states.

This range of activities, if endorsed and implemented, can go a long way toward including the nations of eastern Europe

1. Charles Krauthammer, "Germany: The Big-League Solution," *Washington Post*, June 8, 1990.

and the Soviet Union in a new political and economic system that stretches across all of Europe and across the Atlantic. It can also provide an organization to help resolve the security problems of these nations and serve as a forum for international action. Less obvious but equally important, it can provide a face-saving device to help Soviet leaders obscure how much they have lost, and it can serve at the same time as a cloak to allow the nations of eastern Europe to distance themselves from the Soviet Union without being so obvious about it. In these ways the CSCE can make a major contribution to the stability of a Europe that can be whole and free.

Appendix

CSCE: The Conscience of the Continent

Remarks by Secretary of State James A. Baker III at the CSCE Conference on the Human Dimension, Copenhagen, Denmark, June 6, 1990

We are present at the creation of a new age of Europe.

It is a time of discussion of new architectures, councils, committees, confederations, and common houses.

These are, no doubt, weighty matters.

But all these deliberations of statesmen and diplomats, scholars and lawgivers, will amount to nothing if they forget a basic premise.

This premise is that "all men are created equal, that they are endowed by their Creator with certain inalienable Rights, that among these, are Life, Liberty, and the pursuit of Happiness."

It is "to secure these rights [that] Governments are instituted among them, deriving their just powers from the consent of the governed."

That is why we are here.

Human Rights is a modern phrase. But it recalls the words—and the spirit—of committed men and women throughout Europe's history.

The codes of King Canute.

The Magna Carta.

The Bill of Rights.

The Declaration on the Rights of Man.

The Universal Declaration of Human Rights.

The Helsinki Final Act.

At times over the years these words could not be heard because of yelling crowds, prison gates, and secret police. At times these words have been burned and banned.

But they kept returning on the lips of successor generations.

They could not be destroyed—because they are in the soul of man.

The *very ideas that so stirred Jefferson and Montesquieu resonate today in the words of Havel and Geremek.* They echo in our collective historical memory, and they illuminate our path to the future.

Time and again, we have seen how government's contempt for human dignity led to suffering on an unprecedented scale. Each generation, including ours, has learned what our forefathers discovered—that it is to our collective peril that we close our eyes to the suffering inflicted by intolerance and oppression.

Thomas Jefferson put it this way two hundred years ago: We must swear "upon the altar of God, eternal hostility against every form of tyranny over the mind of man."

And so, today, we, representatives of the people of thirty-five nations, must rededicate ourselves to the cause of human rights; we must reaffirm the democratic values that are our legacy from the past.

We are now closer than ever to realizing the Conference on Security and Cooperation in Europe's (CSCE) long-cherished vision of a Europe whole and free. But as we approach our work, as we consider grand designs and institutional concepts, it is useful to find our bearings by recalling another gathering, fifteen years ago. Then, the peoples of Central and eastern Europe still lived in an artificially divided Europe, isolated behind a wall—a dark curtain, through which the light of world concern reached but dimly.

It was at that dark time, that a band of intrepid men and women in a small flat in Moscow risked their freedom to form the first Helsinki monitoring group. They rejected the darkness of tyranny, and they pledged to bring the denial of human rights to light. Their leader, Yuri Orlov, who is with us now, launched the Helsinki movement with a toast that was as sardonic as it was defiant: "To the success of our hopeless cause!"

Dr. Orlov and his colleagues paid dearly for that pledge. One by one, they were persecuted, arrested, exiled. They all suffered. Some of them died. Yet inspired by their selfless example, one by one, others throughout the Soviet Union and Central and eastern Europe took up the spirit of Helsinki. And one by one, those courageous men and women breathed life into the Helsinki process. They infused the words with meaning.

Before long, these words inspired acts of bravery that dictators and one party states could never comprehend.

In Katowice, in Poland, democratic activists considered the Final Act to be so important that they braved the blows of security forces to distribute copies of it to their neighbors. And it was to the Madrid Meeting of Helsinki signatory states that exiled Solidarity leaders appealed in the aftermath of martial law, proclaiming that there can be no social peace without social justice.

Time and again, Czechoslovakia's Charter '77 cited the Helsinki Final Act in defense of their unjustly persecuted countrymen. They were persecuted for "living in truth," for accepting the praiseworthy folly, as Václav Havel put it, of believing their words and ideals could make a difference. Now, the Charter's original members—President Havel and Foreign Minister Dienstbier to name only two—are leading the new Czech and Slovak Republic to democracy.

When Bucharest's beautiful old buildings were bulldozed and entire villages were threatened by the whim of a dictator, people turned to the CSCE human rights mechanism to spare further destruction of Romania's priceless cultural heritage.

Just before the Berlin Wall fell, scores of East German refugees sought to transit through Hungary to freedom. The reforming Hungarian government, confronted with demands from East German authorities to place old rules in the way of new freedoms, turned to a different set of rules. The Hungarians cited their CSCE obligations to justify the crucial act of safe passage.

And it was the holding in Sofia of a CSCE environmental meeting that coalesced the democratic opposition, precipitating the movement that has brought unprecedented change to Bulgaria.

As we leave the cold war behind us, we confront again many age-old national, religious, and ethnic conflicts that have so sorrowed our common civilization. CSCE, the North Atlantic Treaty Organization (NATO), the European Community (EC), and other democratic institutions of Europe must now play a greater part in deepening and broadening European unity. We must ensure that these organizations continue to complement and reinforce one another.

NATO will continue to serve as the indispensable guarantor of peace—and therefore the ultimate guardian of democracy and prosperity. The alliance will work to lock in stabilizing arms control agreements, to reshape its defense strategy to meet fundamentally changed conditions, and to build bridges of political cooperation to the newly emerging democracies of the East. As President Bush stressed with President Gorbachev at last week's Washington Summit, we believe NATO will remain a cornerstone of both military security and political legitimacy in the new Europe.

Working in concert, the G-24 group of economically developed countries, the Organization for Economic Cooperation and Development, the European Community, the European Bank for Reconstruction and Development, the Council of Europe, the United States, and Canada can foster an inclusive European order, involving Central and eastern European nations and the Soviet Union in the new Europe by assisting market-based reform and the building of democratic institutions.

The prospects for the fulfillment and protection of human rights have never been greater. It is a time for CSCE to take on additional responsibilities—but never at the price of forgetting its fundamental purposes: If CSCE is to help build a new Europe, a Europe different from all those empires and regimes that rose and fell, it must build from the liberty of Man.

Three challenges lie before us:

First, we must ensure that the freedoms so recently won are rooted in societies governed by the rule of law and the consent of the governed.

Second, we must ensure that all peoples of Europe may know the prosperity that comes from economic liberty and competitive markets.

And *third,* we must ensure that we are not drawn into either inadvertent conflict or a replay of the disputes that preceded the cold war.

CSCE is the one forum where our nations can meet on common ground to channel our political will toward meeting these challenges for the entire continent. CSCE's three baskets are uniquely suited to today's political, economic, and security challenges. Though it lacks military or economic power, CSCE can resonate with a powerful and irresistible voice. It can speak to Europe's collective concerns and interests. *It can become, if you will, "the conscience of the continent."*

Deepening our Consensus on Human Rights

Today, I would like to share with you our views on how a strengthened CSCE can meet the first challenge we face: forging a deepened consensus on human rights, political legitimacy through free elections, and the rule of law.

We are all familiar with the Danish author Hans Christian Andersen's tale, "The Emperor's New Clothes." Though written over a century ago, it is an ageless parable. In it, imperious authority cloaks itself in attractive falsehoods, deluding itself in the process. But, in the end, the naked truth is revealed by a small, insistent voice that refuses to be hushed. It grows into a popular cry.

Nineteen eighty-nine was not kind to the Stalinist dictators who cloaked themselves with false authority and ignored the insistent voice and will of the people. Now in Central and eastern Europe, the emerging democracies are working to construct legitimate and enduring political orders. CSCE can help by deepening our consensus on the key building blocks of freedom—genuine elections, political pluralism, and the rule of law.

The new social compacts between government and governed now being written in eastern and Central Europe must be constantly renewed through free elections. As we all know well, democracy—like CSCE—is a *process.* Democracy evolves through give-and-take, consensus-building, and compromise. It thrives on tolerance, where the political will of the majority does not nullify the fundamental rights of the minority.

The free elections proposal that the United Kingdom and the United States tabled last year in Paris has gathered strength from the dramatic events of last fall and the new elections of this spring. In my travels to eastern and Central Europe, democratic activists enthusiastically supported the proposal. They also emphasized the importance they attach to the presence of international observers as their countries undergo the new experience of elections. In February, in Prague, I called upon the CSCE member states to send observer delegations to the elections in eastern and Central Europe. And I am pleased to note that many states have joined us in doing so.

Our revised proposal reflects our experience observing the elections—not only on voting day but also during the electoral campaign. We welcome the strong support that our text is receiving and will work to see it adopted here in Copenhagen. And when the thirty-five consider proposals to institutionalize CSCE, I urge all to start with mechanisms to ensure that governments are freely chosen by the people.

But free and fair elections alone do not ensure that the new democracies will succeed. The irreducible condition of successful democracy, beyond legitimate elections, is clear: fundamental individual freedoms must be guaranteed by restraints on state power. Where these guarantees are absent, there is no *true* democracy. Indeed, where they are absent, the risk of dictatorship always looms.

For this reason, the watchword of reformers everywhere is the rule of law. As the late Andrei Sakharov said, democratic change must be accomplished through democratic methods—peacefully, through legal processes.

But *what do we really mean by rule of law?* The law, after all, has been used as a tool of repression in the societies where rulers make the rules to serve themselves, not the people. As President Bush stressed last month in a speech at the University of South Carolina, the rule of law means the supremacy of laws written through democratic processes, applied in an equal fashion, and upheld by independent judiciaries.

Therefore, we strongly support efforts at this meeting to set forth for CSCE the elements of a democratic society operating under the rule of law. In this regard, President Bush told President Gorbachev how highly we value Soviet efforts to institutionalize the rule of law, *Glasnost'*, and democratization in the USSR.

To this same end, we are engaging in cooperative technical efforts to strengthen democratic political cultures and institutions in Central and eastern Europe.

A closing thought on our human rights agenda: As we turn to the ambitious task of consolidating democracy in entire societies, we must not lose sight of individual liberty. For democracy begins and ends with the citizen and his or her rights. Despite the dramatic gains in human rights that we witness today, men and women in some participating states are still made to suffer because they want to be free, still are targets of intolerance, still cannot emigrate, still may not exercise their full Helsinki rights. We must continue to press until CSCE's high standards of human rights prevail throughout Europe, until they extend to every individual.

Before turning to ways we might strengthen CSCE, I would like to say a word about Lithuania, Latvia, and Estonia. At the Washington Summit, President Bush conveyed our deep misgivings about Soviet policy toward Baltic independence. He stressed again our view that a systematic dialogue must be initiated so that the aspirations of the Baltic peoples can be achieved.

A New Consensus on Strengthening the CSCE Process

The scope for meaningful cooperation in CSCE is widening, and our consensus is deepening in CSCE's human dimension. But in order to have CSCE fulfill its potential in this important area and in CSCE's other baskets, *the Helsinki process itself must be enhanced.*

I recently shared with colleagues *six ideas* on how we can work together to improve CSCE as a process by reinforcing CSCE's organization.

First, the United States favors regular consultations among the signatory states. Ministers may wish to meet at least once a year, and their senior officials should convene at least twice a year. Such exchanges will invigorate the CSCE as a forum for high-level political dialogue.

Second, we support the holding of CSCE review conferences on a more frequent basis, perhaps every two years, and with a fixed duration of about three months.

Third, to ensure that the political commitments we make in CSCE strengthen political legitimacy, we seek *adoption in Copenhagen and confirmation at the Summit of the principle of free and fair elections, political pluralism, and the rule of law.*

Fourth, we seek *confirmation at the Summit of the Bonn Principles of Economic Cooperation.* These principles make clear our mutual commitment to the supportive relationship between political and economic liberty, specifically, thirty-five nations will endeavor to achieve or maintain the free flow of trade and capital, market economies with prices based on supply and demand, and protection for all property including private property and intellectual property.

Fifth, CSCE can play a *major role in dispute management*. We therefore hope that the CSCE summit will reinforce the mandate of the January 1991 Valletta Conference on Peaceful Settlement of Disputes so that it can achieve concrete results. We also believe CSCE can *foster military openness and transparency* through innovative proposals in the Vienna Confidence and Security Building Measures talks, for example, the proposal for a mechanism to request clarification of unusual military activities.

In particular, we believe that CSCE should consider *a mechanism to improve communications among member states*. Our approach might be similar in essence, if not in structure, to the mechanism we have established in the human dimension area as well as to the one which we plan to establish for the Conference on Conventional Forces in Europe (CFE). We should find a way of constructively addressing compliance questions with regard to CSCE security obligations. This might include *observation and inspection reports* in accordance with the Stockholm agreement. We should provide for meetings to exchange information and to discuss the implications of military activities or other unusual occurrences having security implications.

Sixth, I proposed that we begin preparatory work for a possible CSCE summit through a meeting of officials this summer—so I am, of course, pleased that the thirty-five nations have now agreed that our officials will meet next month in Vienna.

I am also pleased that the thirty-five have agreed to our offer to host a CSCE ministerial meeting this fall in connection with the U.N. General Assembly.

Then, *at the CSCE summit, we would expect to sign a CFE agreement*, and President Gorbachev last week indicated he shared this view. At the thirty-five nation summit, we also would expect to review, record, and consolidate progress in all three Helsinki baskets; to strengthen CSCE as a process; and, to plan ahead for the 1992 review conference.

Our work, both before the summit and during it, must also address the subject of *institutionalizing CSCE*.

Until now, CSCE has shown a remarkable ability to both reflect and change with the times. I am confident that it will continue to do so, provided we preserve the flexibility that has made it effective. As we consider proposals for CSCE's development—either for adoption at the summit or for referral by the summit leaders to other upcoming meetings of the CSCE—*the United States will be guided by three key principles.*

One, proposals should reinforce fundamental democratic and market values. *Two,* suggestions for new institutions should complement rather than duplicate roles assigned to existing institutions and fora. And *three,* proposals should result in a stronger trans-Atlantic process of dialogue and consultation regarding Europe's future.

The American delegation to this Copenhagen meeting, which is headed by Ambassador Max Kampelman and which has the complete confidence of President Bush and, of course, myself, will be guided by these criteria.

CSCE: The Conscience of the Continent

I began my remarks with a tribute to the Helsinki monitors who risked their lives and liberty to advance the cause of freedom for others. Many have lived to see the dawn of a much more hopeful day. Some of the monitors are with us in this chamber, and many of them serve as elected representatives of the newly emerging democracies of Central and eastern Europe. *One of the founding monitors of Charter '77* now honors us by leading the distinguished delegation from the Czech and Slovak Federal Republic. *Ambassador Hajek,* you— and your courageous colleagues—are *the very embodiment of CSCE's human dimension.*

You have given this process a heart, a mind, and a searching conscience. *When many viewed CSCE with cynicism, you answered them with dynamism.* You taught us to raise our sights and raise our voices.

The Danish author, Isak Dinesen, was another believer in the power of the human will. One of her favorite mottos was "Je responderay!" I will respond. She lived by that principle, and she was proud to recount how occupied Denmark lived by it during the dark days of the Second World War. The Danish people took it upon themselves to save the entire Jewish community of Denmark—some 8,000 men, women, and children.

By honoring human dignity and the ties that bind all of us, by their efforts and the grace of God, they succeeded beyond all expectation.

Their example is proof positive that commitment of will matters, that responsibility to others matters, and that individual freedoms to act, and think, and feel, can shape not only the moment but the future of one's country.

These same strengths must shape Europe's future. Channeled through CSCE, they can become the conscience of the continent.

Glossary of Terms

Brezhnev Doctrine: A declaration of the right of the Soviet Union to intervene in any "socialist" nation where hostile forces sought to reimpose "a capitalist order" pronounced by Soviet Communist party leader Leonid Brezhnev on November 12, 1968, less than three months after the invasion of Czechoslovakia by Warsaw Pact troops.

Bretton Woods Institutions: They include the International Bank for Reconstruction and Development (World Bank), the International Development Association, the International Finance Corporation, and the International Monetary Fund (IMF). They were established in December of 1945.

"Burden sharing": The term applied to the longstanding debate on both sides of the Atlantic about how much the European allies should contribute to the common defense effort of the Atlantic alliance.

Concert of Europe: Created at the Congress of Vienna in 1815 after the Napoleonic Wars, it was a system conceived by Austrian Foreign Minister Prince Metternich which created a common decisionmaking mechanism for regulating the affairs and disputes of the European countries and protecting the existing order. It lasted in its full form only until 1822.

CFE: Conference on Conventional Forces in Europe. A conference, which opened in Vienna in March 1989, to negotiate the reduction of the conventional forces of NATO and the Warsaw Pact in Europe. There are twenty-three participating countries, members of NATO and the Warsaw Pact, and the conference is placed within the broader security concept of the Helsinki process.

CSBM: Confidence- and security-building measures: A result of the first basket of the Helsinki Accords, these activities are concerned mainly with security issues such as supplying information on military forces and exercises, and communications in times of crisis. Of the review conferences that followed the Helsinki Accords, the one that took place in Stockholm in 1984 was specifically labeled as a Conference on Confidence- and Security-Building Measures.

CSCE: Conference on Security and Cooperation in Europe: A conference process that includes all European countries (except Albania) plus Canada and the United States, a total of thirty-five, and is known informally as the Helsinki process. A product of détente of the early 1970s, the conference first met in Helsinki in 1972 and produced the Helsinki Final Act of 1975. It is not an international organization but a continuing conference that covers European issues ranging from security to economics and human rights.

CoCom: Coordinating Committee for Multilateral Export Controls: An informal multilateral organization through which the United States, its European allies, and Japan attempt to coordinate the national control they apply over the export of strategic materials and technology to communist countries. It was founded in 1950.

CMEA-COMECON: Council for Mutual Economic Assistance: It was founded in 1949 at the initiative of the Soviet Union and includes the members of the Warsaw Pact plus Cuba, Mongolia, and Vietnam. Its aim is to assist the economic development of the member states. After the events of the fall of 1989, three members (Czechoslovakia, Hungary, and Poland) have proposed the dissolution of the organization.

Council of Europe: An organization founded in May 1949 that includes all the countries of Europe except the Warsaw Pact members and Albania. Its seat is in Strasbourg, France, and its aims are to achieve a greater unity among its members, to facilitate their economic and social progress, and to uphold the principles of parliamentary democracy. The Council of Europe has worked mostly in the human rights field. It is expected that the new democracies of eastern Europe will become members soon.

ESOP: Employee Share Ownership Plan: A way to make the employees of a company shareholders with a majority or a minority stake. A means of privatizing state-owned corporations, this approach is under consideration by several governments of eastern Europe.

Eurêka: An organization to coordinate nonmilitary high-technology research that was established by seventeen European countries and the European Community on November 6, 1985, in Hannover, West Germany. It now has twenty-two members and its objective is to coordinate and stimulate the scientific research done in enterprises and research institutes in the field of advanced technologies.

European Bank for Reconstruction and Development: A new bank created to help the democratic governments of eastern Europe convert their economies to market principles. The agreement for its creation was signed on May 30, 1990, and it will start functioning March 1, 1991, with its headquarters in London. Its purpose is to help the East European countries in their efforts to create market economies. Forty countries participate, but the principal shareholders are the members of the European Community, the United States, and Japan.

EC: European Community: Founded by six European countries through the treaties of Paris (1950) and Rome (1957), it has as its primary purpose European economic integration. It currently has twelve members and is based in Brussels. In addition to its economic efforts, the members are presently negotiating the terms of a monetary union and have began to discuss further steps toward political union including the coordination of foreign and security policy.

European Commission: The executive part of the European Community. It has seventeen members from the member states which do not represent their countries but the Community, and its current president is Jacques Delors of France. The members of the Commission head the Community's bureaucracy in Brussels.

EFTA: European Free Trade Association: A group of European states that wanted less economic integration than planned in the European Community. It was established in 1960, and it aims to bring about free trade between member states and other countries in industrial and agricultural goods. It has six members (Austria, Finland, Iceland, Norway, Sweden, and Switzerland) and it is based in Geneva. Most members now want affiliation with or membership in the European Community.

EES: European Economic Space: A concept for associating the EFTA countries with the current plans of the European Community for economic and monetary integration. Although the details are under negotiation currently, the EFTA countries would be part of the integration process and benefit from its results but they will have to accept decisions on trade and monetary policy taken in Brussels without their participation.

European Single Act: The European Single Act is a document signed in February 1986 by the twelve members of the European Community, and it entered into force in June 1987. The act calls for the completion of an integrated internal market by January 1, 1993. It increases the number of decisions that can be made by weighted majority rather than unanimity and increases the power of the European Parliament to amend directives and regulations. It also formalizes European Political Co-operation.

ESA: European Space Agency: Founded in 1975, it has fourteen members (nine from the European Community) and is based in Paris. Its aims are to promote cooperation among European states in space research and technology and their application for peaceful purposes. Its best known projects are the Ariane rocket and the Hermes space shuttle.

Forward Defense: A strategy adopted by the Atlantic alliance in September 1950. Its main point is that any Warsaw Pact aggression must be resisted as far to the East as possible, in order to ensure the defense of all the European member countries. This was especially important in winning political support of the Federal Republic of Germany at the start of the Korean War when the United States and Great Britain wanted to rearm West Germany and admit it to NATO. This strategy required a large conventional force stationed in Germany, and one of its first results was the transfer of four additional army divisions from the United States to Germany.

GATT: General Agreement on Tariffs and Trade: It was founded in 1948 as a multilateral treaty organization aiming to liberalize world trade and place it on a secure basis. It is based in Geneva and has ninety-two members.

"German Question": The problem of how to manage the political, economic, and security affairs of the two German states after 1945 in a way that enhanced the stability of Europe. The

term has taken on new implications since November 1989 as the two German states have moved rapidly toward unification.

Helsinki Final Act: Signed in Helsinki by the thirty-five states participating in the CSCE in 1975 after three years of negotiation. It included sections (baskets) on security in Europe, economic relations between the European states, and human rights. Initially criticized in the West because it recognized the existing borders in eastern Europe, its human rights sections came to be the most widely used. These provisions created trouble for the communist countries when some citizens formed committees for the application of those rights to their countries.

INF: Intermediate-range Nuclear Force negotiations and Treaty: The negotiations started after the dual-track decision of NATO in 1979 to install intermediate-range nuclear missiles in Europe to counter the installation of Soviet intermediate missiles and at the same time to negotiate an arms control agreement to limit these weapons. A final agreement eliminating this category of nuclear weapons from Europe was signed in December 1987 by President Ronald Reagan and General Secretary Mikhail Gorbachev.

NATO: North Atlantic Treaty Organization: It was founded by the Treaty of Washington signed on April 1949. It has sixteen members (fourteen from Europe, Canada, and the United States). The North Atlantic Treaty provides for an international collective defense organization linking the European allies with Canada and the United States.

North Atlantic Council: It is the highest authority of the Atlantic alliance, composed of representatives of the sixteen member states. It meets at the level of Ministers or Permanent Representatives.

Oder-Neisse line: The two rivers that formed the eastern border of Germany after its defeat in 1945. This line meant that territories previously held by Germany would now be part of Poland. Most of the German population of these territories moved to East or West Germany.

OECD: Organization for Economic Cooperation and Development: OECD was founded in 1961, replacing the Organization for European Economic Cooperation (OEEC), which had been set up in 1948 in connection with the Marshall Plan. It constitutes a forum where representatives of the governments of the industrialized democracies attempt to coordinate their economic and social policies. It has twenty-four members and it is headquartered in Paris.

"Open skies": A concept first proposed by President Eisenhower in the 1950s, and subseqently proposed in a revised form by President Bush, it would provide for overflights by unarmed surveillance aircraft to increase transparency and openness and assure compliance with agreements concerning arms control. Negotiations on "open skies" are taking place between the members of NATO and the Warsaw Pact. The first round was in Ottawa in February 1990 and the second in Budapest in April. No agreement has been reached yet.

START: Strategic Arms Reduction Talks: Negotiations between the United States and the Soviet Union regarding long-range nuclear weapons, based on land, at sea, and on bombers. The first round of the START negotiations opened in Geneva in June 1982, replacing the Strategic Arms Limitation Talks (SALT) of earlier administrations. Despite significant progress since 1989, no treaty has been signed.

SNF: Short-range Nuclear Forces: These weapons include battlefield and tactical nuclear weapons with a range of under 500 kilometers. West Germany objected to implementing the NATO decision to modernize the Lance missile and the alliance cancelled that plan in May 1990. The United States has pledged to begin negotiations with the Soviet Union to address the reduction of these weapons after the signing of an arms control agreement on Conventional Forces in Europe (CFE).

TASM: Tactical Air-to-Surface Missiles: First generation tactical nuclear missile. It can strike defended, hardened, and relocatable targets without the aircraft having to overfly the target. It was designed originally for integration on the F-15E and F-111 aircraft but it has the potential for use by the F-16 and the European Tornado aircraft. The system is in the final stages of development.

"Two plus four" talks: Decided in the CSCE meeting in Ottawa in February 1990, they include the two German states and the four victorious powers of World War II (Britain, France, the

Soviet Union, and the United States). The purpose of the talks is to settle the external issues involved in the unification of Germany and to set the terms for ending the four-power rights in both parts of Germany.

Warsaw Pact: The official name of the organization is the Warsaw Treaty of Friendship, Cooperation and Mutual Assistance, and it was founded in May 1955. It was the Soviet answer to the creation of NATO. It has seven members and is supplemented by an interlocking system of treaties between member countries. Its future after the collapse of the communist regimes in most of the member states is a question of speculation, and Hungary has already started the process of withdrawal from the Pact.

WEU: Western European Union. It has nine members (Belgium, France, West Germany, Italy, Luxembourg, Portugal, the Netherlands, Spain, and the United Kingdom), and it is based in London. The WEU is based on the Brussels Treaty of 1948 and was set up in 1955. Its member states seek to harmonize their views on security and defense questions, and it operates in close coordination with NATO.

About the Authors

Josef C. Brada is Professor of Economics at Arizona State University. He received a B.S. and an M.A. from Tufts University and a Ph.D. from the University of Minnesota. Before assuming his post at Arizona State University in 1979, Professor Brada held appointments at New York University's Graduate School of Business Administration and the Ohio State University, and he has been a Visiting Scholar at the Osteuropa Institut in Munich (1984–85). Professor Brada has served since 1987 as a member of the Academic Advisory Committee of the East European Program of the Woodrow Wilson Center. He has authored or edited nine monographs and books, including *The Hungarian Economy in the 1980s: Reforming the System and Adjusting to External Shocks* (1988) and *Economic Adjustment and Reform in Eastern Europe and the Soviet Union* (1989), and written a large number of articles and chapters.

Renata Fritsch-Bournazel is Senior Research Fellow at the Fondation Nationale des Sciences Politiques in Paris and is a former Guest Scholar of the Woodrow Wilson Center. She received a B.A. from the University of Tubingen, an M.A. from the Institut d'Etudes Politiques in Paris, and a Ph.D. from the University of Paris-Sorbonne. Dr. Fritsch-Bournazel teaches at the Institut d'Etudes Politiques in Paris and is the author of numerous works published in French, German, and English. Her books include *L'Union Sovietique at les Allemagnes, Die Französische KP und das Europa-Parlament: Konzeptionen und Aktivitäten,* and *Germany's Role in Europe: Historical and Psychological Dimensions,* and most recently *L'Allemagne: Un Enjeu pour l'Europe.*

Bronisław Geremek is Chairman of the Citizens' Parliamentary Club, an organization that includes both deputies and senators of the Polish Parliament (Solidarity floor leader), Deputy to the Sejm (lower chamber of the Polish Parliament), and Professor of Medieval History at the Institute of History of the Polish Academy of Sciences. Together with Lech Wałęsa, Dr. Geremek founded the Solidarity Trade Union Movement in September 1980. After the imposition of martial law in 1981, he was imprisoned many times for dissident actions. Dr. Geremek received an M.A. from the University of Warsaw and a Ph.D. from the Institute of History at the University of Paris-Sorbonne. Dr. Geremek has published many works in several languages, including *Labor Market in Medieval Paris* (1962) and *History of Polish Culture in the Middle Ages* (1978).

James E. Goodby is Distinguished Service Professor, Department of Engineering and Public Policy, Carnegie-Mellon University. A career diplomat, he served as Deputy Assistant Secretary of State for European Affairs (1977–80), ambassador to Finland (1980–81), vice chairman of the U.S. delegation to START in Geneva (1981–83), and chairman of the U.S. delegation to the Conference on Disarmament in Europe (1983–85). Ambassador Goodby was educated at Harvard University (B.A.) and the University of Michigan.

Steny H. Hoyer is a member of the U.S. House of Representatives (D-Maryland) and Co-Chairman of the Commission on Security and Cooperation in Europe, the organization charged by Congress with monitoring implementation of the Helsinki Accords of the thirty-five-nation Conference on Security and Cooperation in Europe (CSCE). Congressman Hoyer received a B.S. from the University of Maryland and a J.D. from Georgetown University. He is Chairman of the House Democratic Caucus, Vice-Chairman of the House Democratic Steering and Policy Committee, and a member of the House Appropriations Committee.

Max M. Kampelman is a member and former chairman of the Board of Trustees of the Woodrow Wilson Center and Partner at Fried, Frank, Harris, Shriver and Jacobson. Ambassador Kampelman was educated and earned a J.D. at New York University and at the University of Minnesota where he earned a Ph.D. in Political Science. He has served as ambassador and chairman of the U.S. Delegation for the Conference on Security and Cooperation in Europe in Madrid (1980–83), as consultant at the U.S. Department of State (1983–85), as ambassador and head of delegation for the Negotiations on Nuclear and Space Arms in Geneva (1985–88), and as counselor of the

U.S. Department of State (1987–88). He has written on CSCE and arms control issues.

Joseph Kruzel is Acting Director of the Mershon Center for Education and Associate Professor of Political Science at the Ohio State University. Dr. Kruzel's previous positions include special assistant to the Secretary of Defense at the Strategic Arms Limitation Talks (SALT II), and member of the Board of Directors of the Arms Control Association. He has also been a visiting scholar at the Center for Science and International Affairs of Harvard University and a Guest Scholar at the Woodrow Wilson Center. Dr. Kruzel received a B.S. from the U.S. Air Force Academy and an M.P.A. and Ph.D. from Harvard University. He is the author of *Journeys through World Politics* and the editor of *American Defense Annual 1987–88* and *1988–89* and, with Michael H. Haltzel, of *Between the Blocs: Problems and Prospects of Europe's Neutral and Nonaligned States* (1989).

F. Stephen Larrabee is Senior Scholar at the Institute for East-West Security Studies. He was formerly Co-director of the Soviet and East European Research Program at the Johns Hopkins University School of Advanced International Studies in Washington, D.C., and a visiting professor at Cornell University (1982–83). Dr. Larrabee served from 1978 to 1981 on the U.S. National Security Council staff as a specialist on Soviet-East European affairs and East-West political-military relations. From 1977 to 1978 he was a research fellow at the Program for Science and International Affairs, Harvard University. He is the editor of *Technology and Change in East-West Relations* (1989) and *The Two German States and European Security* (1989).

Air Vice Marshal R. A. Mason is Airpower Research Director for the U.K.-based Foundation for International Security. He studied at St. Andrews and London Universities and retired from the Royal Air Force in 1989. For two decades he has lectured internationally on military force in international relations with particular reference to Soviet defense policy and to airpower. He has published many papers and articles and nine books including *Airpower in the Nuclear Age* (1983), *The Soviet Air Force* (1986), *War in the Third Dimension* (1987), and *To Inherit the Skies* (1990).

Alan Milward is Professor of Economic History at the London School of Economics. Professor Milward received his education at the University of London, specifically at University College and the London School of Economics. He specializes in medieval and modern history and in economic history, and has held appointments at the universities of Edinburgh, East Anglia, Stanford, Manchester Institute of Science and Technology, and at the LSE. Professor Milward has written many works, including *War Economy and Society, 1939–1945* (1979), *The Reconstruction of Western Europe, 1945–51* (1984), and numerous articles and chapters.

Péter Paczolay is Counselor at the Hungarian Constitutional Court and Associate Professor of Political Theory at the University of Budapest. He was educated at the University of Budapest where he received a J.D. (1980) and a Ph.D. in Law (1989).

Elizabeth Pond has been European Correspondent, *The Christian Science Monitor*, Bonn (since 1977). She joined the *Christian Science Monitor* in 1965 and has served as its correspondent in Saigon (1967–1969), Tokyo (1971–1974), and Moscow (1974–1976). She has contributed to several journals and newspapers including *Foreign Affairs*, *Problems of Communism*, and *Die Zeit*. Her publications include *From Yaroslavsky Station, Russia Perceived* (1981, latest revision 1988), and she has also contributed chapters to *Indochina in Conflict* (1972) and *Der Gefesselte Riese* (1981). Her awards include the Foreign Press Club Citation in 1982 (for coverage of the European nuclear balance and arms control), and a Twentieth-Century Fund grant (1987–1988) to write a book on "Germany in Détente II." She received her B.A. in International Relations from Principia College and her M.A. in Soviet Union Regional Studies from Harvard University.

Paul W. Schroeder is Professor of European History at the University of Illinois and the author of several books and many articles on European and international politics and Central European history from the eighteenth to the twentieth century. He has been a Woodrow Wilson Center Fellow and serves on the Advisory Council of the West European Program. His current project is a history of the European states system from 1787 to 1848. Professor Schroeder received an

M.A. in History from Texas Christian University (1956) and a Ph.D. in History from the University of Texas (1958). He also studied at the University of Vienna as a Fulbright Scholar.

Viktor S. Shein is Director of Security Studies at the Institute for Europe of the USSR Academy of Sciences. Dr. Shein received a Ph.D. at the Moscow Institute of International Relations. Before joining the Institute for Europe, he was a Senior Fellow at the Institute of the USA and Canada and a member of the Soviet delegation to the Conference on Security and Cooperation in Europe in Vienna in 1987 and 1988. Dr. Shein has written six monographs on NATO and Europe.

Vojislav D. Stanovčić is Professor of Political Theory at Belgrade University, a position he has held since 1968. Professor Stanovčić studied at the Faculties of Law and Philosophy of Belgrade University and earned a Ph.D. degree in Political Science from the Faculty of Law of Belgrade University. In 1988 he was elected Correspondent Member of the Serbian Academy of Sciences and Arts. Professor Stanovčić has written a number of books, studies, and articles, including "History and Status of Ethnic Conflicts" in *Yugoslavia: Fractured Federalism* (1988) and "How Political and Constitutional Institutions Deal with People of Ethnic Diversities" in *Forging Unity Out of Diversity* (1989).

Michael Stürmer is Director of the Research Institute for International Affairs in Ebenhausen, West Germany. Dr. Stürmer has studied history, political science, and philosophy at the Universities of Berlin, London (LSE), and Marburg. He received his doctorate in 1965. Since 1973, he has been full professor of Medieval and Modern History at the Friedrich-Alexander-Universität at Erlangen-Nüremberg, and currently is on long-term leave. Dr. Stürmer has held a number of visiting appointments at universities and institutes around the world. He has written many works, including *Koalition und Opposition in der Weimarer Republik* (1967), *Regierung und Reichstag im Bismarckstaat* (1974), as well as numerous articles on current political and world affairs.

Georges Vaugier is a civil servant of France. He studied at the Sorbonne and the Institut d'Etudes Politiques in Paris.

Samuel F. Wells, Jr. is Deputy Director of the Woodrow Wilson Center. Dr. Wells previously served as Associate Director and directed the European Institute (1985–88) and the International

Security Studies Program of the Woodrow Wilson Center (1977–85). Prior to the creation of that program, he taught international history and defense studies at the University of North Carolina at Chapel Hill. He also served as an author for the major classified study on "The Soviet-American Strategic Arms Competition, 1945–1972" sponsored by the Office of the Secretary of Defense. Recent professional activities include serving as a visiting scholar at the Institut Français des Relations Internationales in Paris. His publications include *The Ordeal of World Power* (1975; co-author), *Economics and World Power: An Assessment of American Diplomacy since 1789* (1984; co-editor), *Limiting Nuclear Proliferation* (1985; co-editor), and *Strategic Defenses and Soviet-American Relations* (1987; co-editor). His contributions to foreign affairs journals include "The United States and European Defense Cooperation" *Survival* (July/August 1985), and "Mitterrand's International Policies" *Washington Quarterly* (Summer 1988). Dr. Wells received his B.A. from the University of North Carolina, and his M.A. and Ph.D. from Harvard University.

Philip D. Zelikow is Director for European Security Affairs on the staff of the National Security Council. He has been a career Foreign Service Officer since 1985, serving first as a political officer at the NATO-Warsaw Pact negotiations on Mutual and Balanced Force Reductions (MBFR) and on the U.S. delegation to the East-West talks on a mandate for new negotiations on Conventional Armed Forces in Europe (CFE), both in Vienna. He then served in the State Department Operations Center and on the Department's Secretariat Staff before assuming his present position. Before joining the State Department, Mr. Zelikow taught for a year at the Naval Postgraduate School in Monterey, California, lecturing on European security and defense issues.

Mr. Zelikow received his B.A. from the University of Redlands, a J.D. from the University of Houston, and an M.A.L.D. from the Fletcher School of Law and Diplomacy at Tufts University. He has held research fellowships at Harvard University's Center for Science and International Affairs and at the International Institute for Strategic Studies. He is the author of articles on European security and national security policy.

"YOU SHALL GO OUT WITH JOY..."